More Praise for *The Marriage Garden*

"A must-have guide for all spouses and anyone who counsels with them. Practical, specific, and wonderfully comprehensive."

—Bob Drewes,
former general officer and
leader of a Fortune 500 business

"*The Marriage Garden* is a delightful book for those looking for tips and advice on how to feed the positives, weed out the negatives, and grow a healthy, flourishing lifelong marriage."

—Melanie Reese,
coordinator, Utah Healthy Marriage Initiative

"I wish this book were longer so that I could continue to feel the joy that each page of the book gave me. I want to shout to each passing couple, 'You have to read this book. It holds the keys to your happiness and joy.' The content is so simple, so profound. There has never been a lovelier garden."

—Dr. George D. Durrant,
author, educator, and husband

"A marriage gold mine for those who really want the best for their marriages."

—Dr. John M. R. Covey,
director of curriculum development,
Marriage, Home and Family,
FranklinCovey Co.

"Most books on marriage today are confusing and theoretical. The clear, practical, and remarkable revelations on cultivating *The Marriage Garden* presented in this concise work should be read, savored, and implemented by all adults wanting more out of their relationships. Whether you are approaching marriage or celebrating your fiftieth anniversary, you will find keys to enriching your marriage within the pages of this book!"

—Steven A. Komadina, MD, FACOG;
past president, the New Mexico State Medical Society;
and two-term New Mexico State Senator

"*The Marriage Garden* is a masterful combination of wisdom, research, and practical examples that can help the reader avoid many marital pitfalls. Its conversational style and engaging questions make it easy to focus on its primary message: in marriage, as with gardening, you reap what you sow."

—David Hanna,
principal, The RBL Group

The Marriage Garden

The Marriage Garden

Cultivating Your Relationship So It Grows and Flourishes

H. Wallace Goddard, PhD, CFLE

James P. Marshall, PhD, LMFT

JOSSEY-BASS
A Wiley Imprint
www.josseybass.com

Published by Jossey-Bass
A Wiley Imprint
989 Market Street, San Francisco, CA 94103-1741—www.josseybass.com

Readers should be aware that Internet Web sites offered as citations and/or sources for further information may have changed or disappeared between the time this was written and when it is read.

Limit of Liability/Disclaimer of Warranty: While the publisher and author have used their best efforts in preparing this book, they make no representations or warranties with respect to the accuracy or completeness of the contents of this book and specifically disclaim any implied warranties of merchantability or fitness for a particular purpose. No warranty may be created or extended by sales representatives or written sales materials. The advice and strategies contained herein may not be suitable for your situation. You should consult with a professional where appropriate. Neither the publisher nor author shall be liable for any loss of profit or any other commercial damages, including but not limited to special, incidental, consequential, or other damages.

Jossey-Bass books and products are available through most bookstores. To contact Jossey-Bass directly call our Customer Care Department within the U.S. at 800-956-7739, outside the U.S. at 317-572-3986, or fax 317-572-4002.

Jossey-Bass also publishes its books in a variety of electronic formats. Some content that appears in print may not be available in electronic books.

Illustrations by Bruce Dupree

Library of Congress Cataloging-in-Publication Data

Goddard, H. Wallace.
  The marriage garden : cultivating your relationship so it grows and flourishes
/H. Wallace Goddard, James P. Marshall.
      p. cm.
  Includes bibliographical references and index.
  ISBN 978-0-470-54761-8 (pbk.)
1. Marriage. I. Marshall, James P., date. II. Title.
  HQ734.G586 2010
  646.7'8—dc22   2009050430

Printed in the United States of America
FIRST EDITION
PB Printing   10 9 8 7 6 5 4 3 2 1

Contents

Acknowledgments

We are grateful to the team of amazing people with whom we work at the University of Arkansas Division of Agriculture Cooperative Extension Service. Traci Johnston, Sherry Jones, Katy Randall, Lindsey Smith, and Jennie Hubbard were a part of the team when we started the Marriage Garden project. Since then we have benefited from the work and insight of Melissa Potter, Chris Hughes, Katie Baney, and Rebecca Simon. We thank Lynn Russell and Anne Sortor, our two administrators, who encouraged us along the way. All these good people have contributed immensely to our efforts.

Thanks to the hard-working Jossey-Bass people who contributed so much to this book, including Alan Rinzler, Nana Twumasi, Carol Hartland, Jennifer Wenzel, and Donna Cohn.

We offer special thanks to our artist and friend, Bruce Dupree, who made the garden so inviting with his lush illustrations.

We are also grateful to the good friends and family members who have shared their stories and insights. Life experience is the best source of discovery and learning, and many people have generously shared their experiences with us.

We thank the University of Arkansas Division of Agriculture Cooperative Extension Service. Extension Service is built on a great idea—that the best discoveries of research should be made available to all Americans so that they can live better lives. We are glad to be part of a system with such a noble mission.

We thank the excellent scholars who have built the field of relationship strengthening from a marginal and speculative field to a first-class research enterprise.

We thank our spouses and families. They patiently forgive us and lovingly encourage us as our actions labor to catch up to our knowledge.

We thank you, the reader, for your interest in building and supporting strong relationships. We hope that more and more people will learn and use those principles that can make for vibrant relationships.

A Note from the Authors

The *Marriage Garden* is based on the Marriage Garden curriculum that was created by H. Wallace Goddard and James P. Marshall of the University of Arkansas Division of Agriculture Cooperative Extension Service.

As you read *The Marriage Garden*, you will hear the voices of both authors speaking to you in the first person as well as blending together at times. Each of us was the primary author on certain chapters and a contributing author on the others. In those chapters where we are the primary author, we use the first names of our wives, children, siblings, parents, families, and friends from time to time. They are an integral part of our gardening team. You will hear Wally speak fondly of the goodness in his dear wife, Nancy. You will hear James speak often of the compassion and creativity of his dear wife, Kathie. Both of us will also be making reference to our parents and children, family and friends, couples we've worked with, and other folks we know and care about.

We look forward to meeting you in the Marriage Garden. And we would love to have you share your stories as you apply the principles of commitment, growth, nurturing, understanding, problem solving, and serving with us at MarriageGarden@uaex.edu.

The Marriage Garden

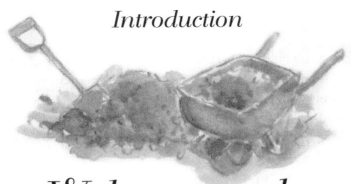

Welcome to the Marriage Garden!

The University of Arkansas sponsors a botanical garden not far from our home. It is breathtaking! Under the protection of a forest canopy, Nancy and I meander along the winding paths, enjoying a profusion of colors. The giant trees shelter the 210-acre peninsula and the magical paths on Lake Hamilton from the world. The Japanese maples soften the landscape. Streams and ponds invite quiet reflection. Magnificent blooms inspire awe.

Each season shares unique riches with visitors. Winter offers its camellias; spring its daffodils, azaleas, and dogwoods. Summer is enriched with wildflowers and roses. In the fall, the garden catches fire with vibrant leaf colors. It's hard to imagine that the Garden of Eden was any lovelier than Garvan Woodland Gardens.

As Nancy and I sat on a bench overlooking the verdant gardens during a recent visit, the beauty all seemed so natural and effortless. Nature smiled. We surrendered to peace. At such times there is no hint of the army of trained specialists who care for the gardens. Hundreds of people invest thousands of hours every month to make the garden Edenic. They watch for pests, spray for

1

blights, plant bulbs, prune branches, and fertilize steadily. An army of trained professionals makes the garden look perfectly natural. Yet we blissfully enjoy peace, quite heedless of the efforts that make our serenity possible.

The Marriage Garden

There's a good reason we compare marriage to a garden. A good marriage is as lush, rich, and satisfying as a great garden. But neither the good marriage nor the great garden happens without wise and consistent effort. Marriage, like a garden, can be renewing and life sustaining. Yet neither will happen by accident.

There are many things that amateur gardeners do that are ineffective or even counterproductive. For example, the popular practice of smearing black sealer on a pruning wound is a bad idea. It inhibits the tree's own healing process and may even provide a place for disease to grow. Still, the practice persists. Many people feel compelled to cover any tree wound with some chemical bandage.

There are many popular marital remedies that are similarly ineffective or even counterproductive. For example, many people believe that the key to marital success is the sharing of discontents in ways that are fair. The assumption is that we must let our partners know what changes are needed if we are ever to have the relationships we want. This practice not only fails to enrich a relationship, but it regularly creates a spiral of fault-finding that can doom a relationship.

Common sense is not always good sense. That is why it has required decades of intensive research on marriage to provide the key to building strong relationships. Research shows us where common sense is nonsense. We want to do the things that strengthen our relationships rather than destroy them. Doing the wrong things with good intentions is still likely to have harmful consequences.

This book is focused on six processes that research has shown to make marriages flourish. Each chapter considers one of those processes and shows how you can make your marriage blossom like a magnificent rose by applying that chapter's process in your romantic relationship. It may surprise you to find that when you do the right things, you can actually have a better marriage—with less effort than needed to do the usual things that you thought would help.

That doesn't mean that a good marriage happens without effort. It only means that we sometimes invest herculean efforts in doing the wrong things. We want to help you do the right things. And before we even begin to talk about those six key processes, we want to share some basic rules for gardeners. These principles are somewhat like the rules that Garvan Gardens would give you before making a tour of the gardens. They might ask you to avoid pulling up any flowers, stomping off the designated paths, or littering.

We want to provide you with six tips that will make your trip through *The Marriage Garden* safer and more enjoyable. These six guiding principles are worth remembering every time you think about your relationship. These principles will prepare you to enter *The Marriage Garden* and learn the processes to cultivate a vibrant, flourishing garden.

Remember the Guiding Principles

See the Good

Our lives and relationships are packed with a mixture of complaints, joys, disappointments, and satisfactions. There are bruised sensibilities and battles about toilet seats, facial hair, body odors,

3

and noises. There are also times of fun, laughter, closeness, and joy. Both negative and positive experiences are entirely natural.

Because of the mixture of good and bad, it is quite natural to think that we must be continuously pulling weeds from our partners' souls. If we fail to be vigilant, the weeds may take over! Yet the master gardeners we know tell us that the best way to deal with weeds is to grow healthy, desirable plants to shut out the weeds. The same is true in marriage.

According to research, the key to healthy relationships is not the constant attention to weeds and pesky behavior. We may think that we'll build a better relationship by dealing with our discontents. But this keeps the focus on the problems. When we focus on our discontents, we are likely to get stuck in them. And, after pulling the weeds, we're still likely to have bare earth—that is, even if we could get our partners to stop doing the things that annoy us, we would have partners who are dispirited and discouraged. They will have stopped being themselves.

The surest way to make progress toward building a vibrant marriage is to plant strong and healthy plants. Let them crowd out the annoyances—if not in reality then at least in our minds. Notice what you've done that *has* been satisfying and enjoyable. Focus on the good in your marriage!

Let me give you an example. Nancy and I (Wally) had not been married very long when I noticed that she sometimes left things on the kitchen counters. She seemed like a decent human being, yet she would leave a jar of peanut butter sitting out. I wondered what was wrong with her. Early in our relationship, I tried telling Nancy things like, "Honey, I really appreciate a tidy kitchen. Do you mind putting away the peanut butter after you use it?" In spite of my perfectly reasonable request, Nancy seemed to feel hurt. She put away the peanut butter, but her spirits seemed to sag. And a few days later, peanut butter would again be left on the counter.

Finally—years later—I realized that it didn't bother Nancy to have a few items left on the counter. It bothered me for some reason. (Am I a perfectionist? Did I learn some arbitrary family rules in my childhood?) So I learned a priceless lesson: If the peanut butter bothered me, I could put it away.

Please don't misunderstand me. We can make requests and express preferences to our partners. But if they know about our preferences and still don't act on that knowledge, then we can take responsibility. We don't need to dwell on the weeds when we can plant a vibrant plant in its place. I can, for example, thank Nancy for the peanut butter fudge she makes for me. And I can put away the peanut butter myself.

When we are mindful and thankful for all the good things our partners do, they are happier, we are more peaceful, and the relationship flourishes. So don't dwell on irritations. Instead, think about and talk about all the good things that are a part of your relationship.

Reflection

This idea is likely to be more helpful to you if you take a few minutes to reflect on these questions:

- What does your partner do that brightens your life?
- When you run into irritations, what can you do to minimize or remove them?

Notice Your Feelings

Some thoughts and experiences help us feel more peaceful and happy. Others make us more tense and angry. Feelings provide us vital clues.

If we dwell on the thoughts and feelings that make us angry, we are likely to get angrier. It's a predictable path. Something bothers us. We try to understand it. We look for related experiences. Pretty soon we conclude that our partners are messed up. We will probably feel an urge to lecture them or avoid them.

In contrast, if we privilege our positive feelings—if we dwell on them and trust them—we are likely to get happier. Positivity snowballs. We feel grateful for our partners, we act more kindly, and the relationship grows. We find ever more positives.

Every day that we are together with our spouses we have plenty of opportunities to feel positively or negatively toward them. Every day they will do things that could annoy us. Every day they will do things that could please us. We can choose which ones to honor with our attention, reflection, and comments.

You can see how much this is like gardening. If we want some weeds to die, we can cut them off from light and water. If we want flowers to grow, we can be sure that they get our attention. When they begin to wilt, we can be angry at them. We can wish we had never bought them. Or we can water them.

One of the clearest findings of research on marriage is that partnerships grow when we focus on the positive.

We have friends who have only been married a few months. They come from very different backgrounds. He comes from an easygoing family in a small town. She comes from an intense family and works in the fashion industry. If you're pretty perceptive, you can anticipate what challenges they are facing. He doesn't worry much about appearances and acts in ways that annoy his wife. She pesters him about it, but she might as well be asking a rose bush to grow rutabagas as to ask her husband to be as style-conscious as she is. It just doesn't matter to him. So she spends a fair amount of time being annoyed and he keeps wondering why his wife is upset. She is especially likely to get upset with her husband when she feels tired, stressed, or sick.

Our prediction is that there will be a lot of hurt feelings through the first years of marriage. Eventually she may realize that her husband's easygoing ways are a perfect complement to her intensity and perfectionism. They are an invitation for her to relax. As the years go by, he may become more aware of ways he can adjust to please his wife. Because they are both good people, we predict that they will develop a strong marriage.

But if they dwell on the irritations, they will become more and more unhappy. They may divorce. Or they may stay together and be miserable. Yet, if they decide to look for the good and dwell on it, their marriage will get better and better.

Reflection

Take a few minutes to respond to these questions:

+ Think of a time when you were tempted to be irritated with your spouse and you chose to see the good instead. Maybe you realize that this is a choice. Are you prepared to see the good next time something goes wrong?
+ Feelings are the result of our thoughts. What thoughts help you to have positive feelings toward your spouse and your marriage?

Speak from Peace

The things we say when we are upset may feel powerful and authentic. Suddenly it seems so perfectly clear that our spouses are self-centered cads! So we tell them off and figure that they ought to be grateful that we are so perceptive and honest. We will fix their pocked souls. We may feel quite noble as we fuss with our spouses' characters.

The trouble is that most spouses don't want to be fixed; they want to be loved. As we start to diagnose partner maladies and prescribe wise solutions, our spouses are glad to tell us where we are mistaken. They know that some of our characterizations are simply flawed. And they probably have some ideas about what is wrong in our souls—which they are glad to share with us. Pretty soon we have angry partners clubbing each other with partial truths.

It turns out that anger can make fools of the best of us. Instead of seeing the big picture with personal struggles and imperfections mixed with life events, anger focuses us on a specific assault on our view of right and wrong. We ignore mountains of truth to focus on a tiny problem.

That's why angry discussions are usually not very productive. When we're feeling angry, disappointed, hurt, and resentful, we are likely to say and do things that aren't fair *and* that hurt the relationship.

We all get upset. We all say destructive things. But we don't have to make fools of ourselves. We can calm ourselves down. This can be a difficult task. Sometimes we feel that we absolutely *must* say what is on our minds. But we can have just enough presence of mind to say to ourselves, "I'm sure there is a good reason they acted that way." As we set aside our accusations and start to take our partners' points of view, a hint of peace can sneak into our souls.

By breathing deeply and thinking peaceful thoughts, we prepare ourselves to share in a helpful way.

Sometimes it's wise to say, "Right now I am upset. I would like to take some time to think about my feelings so I can express myself in a way that is fair to you." Or maybe you say, "Give me some room. I'm not ready to talk." Once we have claimed some time, it is vital to use it not to amass evidence of our spouses' guilt but to regain our bearings on life. For example, puttering around in the backyard pulling a few weeds or enjoying the sounds of the neighborhood can help us settle down.

The wisdom of this course is easy to demonstrate. You have almost surely had someone very mad at you some time in your life. Maybe it was your spouse or a parent or a boss or a neighbor. When that person was chewing you out, did you reflect quietly, "Ahh. Good point. I really would like to do better at that"? I bet you didn't. I bet you felt insulted and angry and mentally prepared your own counterattack. Lecturing people doesn't make them wiser, it just makes them mad. And it damages relationships.

Instead of attacking and destroying our partners with angry accusations, we can speak from peace and thus bring our different perspectives together to build a stronger relationship.

Reflection

Take a few minutes to respond to these questions:

+ What helps you calm down when you are upset?
+ Do you see irritation coming? What can you do to see your partner's point of view rather than let irritation separate you?

Weed Your Own Garden

A gardener planted a tree along the edge of his property. He nurtured it and cherished it. But his next-door neighbor disliked the tree. It did not interfere with his home, his view, or his driveway. He just didn't like the tree. As branches grew over his property, he complained to the neighbor about the tree. The gardener was amazed. He loved the tree. The two simply could not agree on the tree. One evening the tree hater got out his ladder and a pruning saw and cut off all the branches that overhung his property. The stark, half-stripped tree stood as a monument to a neighbor's inability to make small allowances for someone else's preferences.

In many ways, this real story provides a fitting metaphor for marriage. Every couple has differences. And some of those differences bother us. You might argue that branches hanging into your life are an intrusion into your space.

You're right. But the big problem is not those branches. It is the irritation. If I am the tree-resenting neighbor, I stop noticing the flowers I planted and the shrubs that are blooming. All I think about is that darned tree and its intrusion into my life. If I invested as much energy into caring for my own yard as I did in resenting the bothersome tree, my yard would likely flourish.

You can see how this applies to the regular irritations of marriage. There are trees growing in our spouses' soul that bother us. Maybe my spouse is untidy. Maybe she wears funny shoes. Maybe she uses too much ketchup or talks with her mouth full. There is sure to be something. In every relationship, there are plenty of reasons to be bothered.

We like the way Irving Becker described the human dilemma: "If you don't like someone, the way he holds his spoon will make you furious; if you do like him, he can turn his plate over into your lap and you won't mind."

We can choose to be irritated with our spouses. Or we can choose to busily care for our own flowerbeds.

We can spend a lot of time trying to prune our partners' ways or we can invest our energy in making our yards flourish. We can cultivate patience, plant kindness, nurture compassion.

Reflection

Take a few minutes to respond to these questions:

+ Can you think of a time when you were tempted to find fault with your partner but chose instead to "weed your own garden"— in other words, find ways to be a better partner yourself? How did that choice change your mood and relationship?
+ Irritation is the common seedbed for criticism. What helps you manage or reduce irritation?

Manage Expectations

Early in the relationship, romantic feelings may set our expectations. We assume that a healthy relationship will always be filled with laughter, surprise, and passion. When those feelings diminish (as they always do) or are eclipsed by irritation, we start to wonder if we made a bad choice. Maybe this relationship just doesn't have the magic.

The reality is that romance gets us together but cannot keep us together. Within a couple of years in a relationship, it becomes clear that our partners have significant flaws *and* that those flaws are not going away—even with our persistent prodding. This can be very disenchanting. We can increase our demands for change in our partners. We can put our energy into other areas of our lives. Or we can manage our expectations.

When we increase demands for partner change, we are likely to elicit a counteroffensive. Our partners are generally quite glad to show us that all the relationship problems are due to *our* selfishness and unreasonable demands. Conflict escalates.

When we give up on our marriages and put our energy into other areas of our lives, our marriages become dead shells. They are like the skin left behind by a molting garden snake when it sheds its skin. They have the form of a marriage but no life.

There is a third alternative. We can manage our expectations. We can help them mature from romance to companionship—which is a much more stable place. It may have fewer fireworks but has more satisfaction. In fact, research shows that we must build companionship if we want our relationship to outlast the romantic phase.

Marriage follows the law of the harvest, which states that only patient, wise effort over time will result in a good crop. You cannot pick juicy, ripe tomatoes a week after planting a seedling. You cannot grow a strong marriage in even a month of earnest effort. It takes time. But that patient effort over time can result in an incredible harvest.

There is another key to managing expectations. When we demand that marriage meet all our needs and make us happy, we are much like an infant who throws a fit when fed strained carrots instead of chocolate pudding. It is no wonder that people like chocolate pudding. But unless we are willing to welcome vegetables into our lives, we are likely to languish. When we think of marriage as a day at a carnival, we are sure to be disappointed.

12

When we think of marriage as more like working in a garden, we are likely to have a lovely garden and deep satisfaction.

"Strained carrots!" you may say. Who wants to be married if marriage is a steady diet of strained carrots? OK. So strained carrots aren't very appealing for most of us. But we hope there are fruits and vegetables that you do like. A healthy marriage is a little like a healthy, balanced diet. Just as each of us must make place for a variety of healthy foods if we want to flourish, so too can we select the parts of our partners' characters that delight us, and we can make these the centerpiece of our relationship. We can stew over our partner's forgetfulness or we can enjoy her spontaneity.

We manage expectations when we train ourselves to notice and appreciate the good things in our partners' characters and in our relationships. We also expect that there will be surprises that challenge us occasionally. We see them as invitations to growth. Managing expectations is not so hard. But we shouldn't order Caesar salad and then get mad that it doesn't taste like chocolate crème brulée. Rather, we can appreciate our partners' strengths and stay open to new discoveries.

Reflection

Take a few minutes to respond to these questions:

+ Can you think of a time when you have patiently worked at something and been richly rewarded for your efforts? How can that apply to your marriage relationship?
+ What are the roses in your relationship? How can you better accept the thorns that come with the roses?

When Your Soul Speaks, Take Great Notes

Just as we would take a picture of an amazing flower in our gardens or make a record of the plants that worked well, so too should we make a record of sweet truths that settle in on us. The record might be a sentence or two describing our discovery. It might be a few words celebrating the goodness we have seen or experienced, or a journal entry recording the things we appreciate about our partners. It might even be a doodle or sketch that reminds us of what we felt. It could be a photograph that captures the joy of the occasion.

When you suddenly see blessings in your relationship, observe strengths in your partner, or feel love, closeness, and compassion for your partner, make a record of the thought and feeling. Making the record not only helps you cement the memory but also provides a practical and effective way to carry all your good experiences of the past into the present.

As you read *The Marriage Garden*, we hope your soul will speak to you, at least a time or two, about ideas and practices that will bless and strengthen your relationship. When it does, we invite you to take great notes and then take action.

Reflection

Take a few minutes to respond to these questions:

•   How do you currently feel blessed by your partner? Write it down.
•   What good experiences have you had together in the last few weeks?

So, before you even step foot in the garden, make sure that you have these guiding principles in mind. They will help you turn your dreams of a happy marriage garden into a reality. Maybe you will want to revisit these principles before you undertake a relationship discussion.

With these guiding principles, you are ready to learn the lessons of effective marriage gardening. Each of the next six chapters introduces a new principle, discusses its application, and helps you prepare to be a better gardener. The concluding chapter discusses how you can bring the six principles together to become a master gardener and reap a glorious marital harvest.

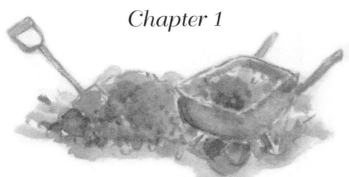

Chapter 1

Commitment

The Choice to Pledge Your Best Efforts

In marriage, the grass grows greener on the side of the fence you water most.

—James Marshall

You're in the backyard or a neighborhood park trying to relax and enjoy some peaceful time. But there are no healthy trees, the sun is scalding you, the bugs are buzzing you, and there just isn't much to look at.

You look around. You love flowers. You dream of flower beds packed with color. You yearn for some wildflowers along the fence. But what you see looks more like an RV parking lot than a botanical garden.

Cultivating Your Garden

Every once in a while you dream of raising a few herbs and vegetables—maybe a little basil and some robust tomatoes. But every time you've tried, the bugs and birds have enjoyed a feast while you have been exasperated.

It's discouraging. Your hopes and dreams are worlds apart from the dreary reality you see before you.

Imagine that something stirs inside you. You stiffen your resolve and march down to the local mom-and-pop or big box superstore. There you find a rack filled with colorful seed packets as vibrant as life. Or you're thrilled to find bins filled with bulk seeds from amaranthus to zucchini. You feel optimism building in your soul.

You grab a handful of packets and even get a pound of rutabaga seeds; you can't stand rutabaga, but the seeds are so interesting! You pay the cashier and head home. You get back to your barren patch, whether it's in your backyard or a block away at a few square yards of available park land, and heartless reality confronts you. Exactly how will you turn this parched plot into a verdant refuge? You now remember the shovels, compost, fertilizers, and so forth that filled the shelves at the store. Maybe you should have taken these gardening aspirations a little more seriously.

Yet you refuse to be intimidated. You grab a handful of precious seed. With a flourish you toss the seed toward the wasteland. You do the same with the next bag of seed. And the next. You have a nagging feeling that this may not be the way to guarantee a glorious garden. Some of the seeds may not take root, but at least it's a step in the right direction. You empty all the bags of seed over the parched soil and weeds.

Then you head back to the living room. You turn on the television, hoping to calm those nagging feelings about shovels, plans, watering, and fertilizing. You're willing to give Mother Nature a chance to show what she can do.

18

Disappointing First Results

Let's turn the calendar ahead two or three months. You decide it's time to check on your garden. So you head over to the seed patch hoping to survey the lush vegetation and harvest some early crops. But as you arrive at the garden, you're surprised to find no hint of new growth (except maybe some fat birds that appear to have been enjoying a feast). If anything, the wannabe garden spot looks more desolate than before. You scratch your head. Oh, well. Maybe you can try again next summer.

What Is the Marriage Garden?

Great gardens are not happy accidents. They are the result of careful planning, thorough preparation, and steady attention. We may take some workshops, consult books, check with neighbors, and quiz our county agricultural agent or other local experts in order to make a plan. We spend time testing and preparing the soil. We choose plants carefully. We tend them consistently— watching for bugs and applying fertilizer as needed. We try things out and see if they work, as every garden has its own unique topographic character, soil quality, and microclimate. And the successful gardener remembers to water regularly.

Maybe you can see the similarity of our gardening failures to our disappointments in marriage. Most of us enter the most important and challenging relationship of a lifetime without taking a single class to prepare us. Most of us read nothing more substantial than a romance novel to help us design our relationships. Most of us don't try to acquire the necessary tools to help us.

We usually don't have much of a plan for making the most of our little plot of love. Then, after we have thrown ourselves into marriage, we do not continue to water the plants or watch studiously for bothersome pests. We just settle into an easy chair and wait for a lush relationship.

It's not going to happen. Great relationships don't happen by accident.

Of course, romance can seem both easy and lush—at the beginning. But this first flush of intense and passionate emotion will not last forever, and is not what sustains a long-term relationship. It is more like the bridal bouquet at a wedding reception than the rich plant life that we hope will fill our yards.

Cultivating a great garden requires commitment at the beginning and commitment in the day-to-day work that makes a garden grow. Some people will be discouraged by the weeds and pests. But those who hang in there and who make and sustain a commitment will enjoy a lovely garden.

To have that lovely garden requires wise and steady effort over time. Healthy relationships also require this kind of commitment.

Healthy Commitment

Let's savor a story of healthy commitment and then talk about the essential elements of commitment.

I admire John Glenn. He is duly famous for his work as a test pilot, astronaut, politician, and again as an astronaut later in life. I admire him most for his work as a husband.

John and his wife, Annie, grew up together. They played together as children and dated through high school. John described Annie as "pretty, with dark hair and a shy, bright smile."

They were in band, glee club and YMCA/YWCA together. They were devoted friends to each other.

But there were challenges. Some of their classmates teased Annie for her severe stuttering. But John didn't see her stuttering as a problem. "It was just something she did, no different from some people writing left-handed and others right-handed. I thought it was cruel and thoughtless to laugh at someone for something like that—especially Annie, whom I cared for—and I told them so."

Annie's stuttering made it almost impossible for her to do many things, including shopping. She would need to have someone else along to do the talking or write a description of what she wanted and show it to a clerk. Any public appearance was painful for Annie. Yet John lived a very public life.

At one point when John was on the brink of his first space launch, he got an urgent message from flight control to persuade his wife Annie to go along with a political PR event. When he asked his superior officer what it was all about, he learned that Vice President Johnson wanted to visit their home. Annie refused. John had been pressured with the threat that his place in the space program could be in jeopardy if he did not cooperate.

This is a situation where most of us might have fared poorly as husbands. We might have called our wives and said, "Look, I'm risking my life for the country—can't you simply step out of your comfort zone and meet with the vice president for a few minutes?" But John Glenn was different. "Annie wouldn't have refused to see the vice president without a really good reason. I called her, and she said Johnson wanted to bring in network television cameras and some of the reporters who were camped outside. She said she was tired, had a headache, and she just wasn't going to allow all those people in her house. I told her whatever she wanted to do; I would back her 100 percent."

Wow! John was mindful and respectful of his wife's feelings even when they caused him inconvenience. His commitment to Annie exceeded his commitment to his career.

Years later John Glenn was considered as a running mate for Jimmy Carter. Reportedly he was not chosen in part because of Annie's stutter. "It shocked us and it hurt." But, out of the political race, John Glenn joked that he was free to mow the lawn at home.

At one point later in life, Annie took an intensive course to help her overcome stuttering. After the three weeks of grueling training, she called home.

John described the conversation:

"John," she said on the line from Virginia, forming her words slowly and carefully, "today we went to a shopping center and went shopping. And I could ask for things. Imagine that."

I had never heard Annie speak that many words without a single pause. It was all I could do to reply, "That's wonderful!"

"I think so, too," she said slowly. "It's a start."

Annie grasped the gift of speech and held it tight. Our lives were transformed. "John," she said when she got home, hiding an impish smile, "I've wanted to tell you this for years: Pick up your socks."

Our phone bill increased as she started calling friends around the country. She had never been able to read children's stories to Lyn and Dave (our children) when they were little.

John Glenn might have been irritated many times by Annie's stuttering, her quietness, and the impact that her disability had on his life and career. But he wasn't. Instead he loved his Annie. He helped her. He saw past her impediment to the woman he loved. He was devoted to her.

If I had a chance to interview John Glenn, I would be less interested in knowing about the sights and sensations of outer space and more about the workings of his inner space. How did he learn to cultivate the garden of his marriage? What lessons in life prepared him to be loving and considerate even when it was inconvenient? How did he learn commitment? Did he ever feel irritated and have to stifle the urge to blame? What enabled him to see Annie in tender and loving ways even when he may have wished things were different?

Problems with Commitment

Most of us aren't as good at commitment as John Glenn. In fact, many sociologists have observed that in our society, relationship commitment is a yellow and wilting plant. The leaves are falling to the ground.

Roy Baumeister, the perceptive and famous psychologist, has written insightfully about a cultural shift that makes it much harder for marital commitment to survive in our society. He suggested that our cultural heroes have traditionally been people who sacrificed themselves for the well-being of others. Heroes set aside their own convenience and preferences in order to rescue a drowning child, protect a threatened family, or protect an attacked community. In contrast to heroes, villains have been the people who met their own needs above all others.

According to Baumeister, "[M]orality has become allied with self-interest. It is not simply that people have the right to do what is best for them (although that is an important part of it); rather, it has become an almost sacred obligation to do so. The modern message is that what is right and good and valuable to do in life is to focus on yourself, to learn what is inside you, to express and cultivate these inner resources, to do what is best for yourself, and so forth."

Baumeister wrote: "Survey researchers in the 1950s found that people tended to judge the self by its ability to make and maintain a marriage. By the 1970s, this was reversed: Marriages were judged by the contribution to the self, including increases in self-expression, happiness, and well-being. In fact, if a relationship does not bring pleasure, insight, satisfaction, and fulfillment to the self, then it is regarded as wrong, and the individual is justified— perhaps even obligated—to end the relationship and find a new, more fulfilling one."

What was once considered selfish and egotistical is now a moral imperative. We must take care of ourselves. This cultural shift is much like a climate change that makes it much harder for the delicate plants of marital commitment to survive under the demands of self-interest.

Why Should We Cultivate Our Marriage Garden?

Despite the big cultural trends, most of us still yearn to be thoughtful, helpful, and considerate. We value unselfishness in ourselves and others. Yet we may have made a subtle change in the questions we ask ourselves. The traditional heroes might have asked: *What's the right thing for me to do?*

Today we are more likely to ask: *How can I be in this relationship if it's not good for me?*

The latter question seems reasonable enough, yet it harbors a couple of subtle—and commitment-damaging—assumptions. First, it assumes that we can rightly assess the value of our marriage when we feel distressed. Research shows that the same biased perception that caused people to fall in love and ignore many challenges gets turned on its head when a relationship is distressed. At such times we see unrelenting badness and we ignore or undervalue the good.

Second, the idea that marriage must meet all our most fundamental needs puts a terrible burden on the relationship. It's like asking your Honda Accord to carry a couple of tons of lumber for building your backyard deck. The Accord was not designed for such duty. And marriage was not designed to meet all our needs.

It's impossible and unhealthy to expect a garden or a marriage to be the only source of everything we require for ultimate survival and happiness. In the case of marriage there's no way our beloved wives or husbands can or should be responsible for every one of our wants, needs, pleasures, satisfactions, connections, and identity in the universe. The institution of marriage is groaning under such crushing expectations.

What Can Marriage Provide?

Jonathan Haidt has wisely observed that we often make major life decisions while under the influence of temporary emotions. He compares passionate love to alcohol or marijuana. Such drugs make us high. But we can't sustain that high. We crash. He warns: "People are not allowed to sign contracts when they are drunk, and I sometimes wish we could prevent people from proposing marriage when they are high on passionate love because once a marriage proposal is accepted, families are notified, and a date is set, it's very hard to stop the train. The drug is likely to wear off at some point during the stressful wedding planning phase, and many of these couples will walk down the aisle with doubt in their hearts and divorce in their future."

The best of marriages—those that are ultimately satisfying and enduring—provide two things: sweet companionship and opportunities to grow. The passion that got most people married—and that many people yearn for—is a temporary insanity. It was never designed to sustain relationships over time. Let's return to our garden metaphor. A good garden will thrill us when we first enjoy the seeds and blossoms, and then it provides a place to relax and enjoy peaceful moments. It will give us many opportunities to learn responsibility, consistency, and awareness. The garden is not likely to provide the thrills of an amusement park, the fitness promised by the gym, or the livelihood that takes you to the workplace. The same is true of marriage. Marriages provide solid benefits when we steadily care for them, but they do not meet all our needs.

Reflection

Take a few minutes to respond to these questions:

• What are some of the qualities that first attracted you to your partner? Do you still see and appreciate them? What are you doing or what can you do to remain mindful of them?

+ What have you invested toward creating a vibrant marriage garden of your relationship? As you listen to your heart, what more do you feel you would like to do to make your marriage flourish?

Different Kinds of Commitment

Scholars who study commitment talk about three kinds of commitment. The first is attraction. This might be called the "want to" commitment because a person is drawn toward the partner. Some people are committed to a relationship because of the sexual rewards and satisfactions of the relationship. Maybe he sees her as beautiful, charming, intelligent, and capable. She may see him as kind, capable, and good-hearted. This kind of commitment can help sustain a relationship—if we continue to focus on the attractive elements of our partners after the thrill of first flush. This kind of attraction fails if we let familiarity crowd out appreciation.

A second kind of commitment is moral obligation. This can be called the "ought to" kind of commitment. Some people stay in a relationship even when it is challenging because they see it as a vow, an obligation, or a duty. For many people, commitment to marriage is a vital part of their religious or family values.

Christensen and Jacobson tell this story about Abraham Lincoln.

> Lincoln was outside talking to a congressman about the important political matters of the day when his wife Mary Todd Lincoln stormed out of the house, ruthlessly castigated Lincoln for something he had done, and then

stormed back inside. Aghast that a wife would behave so outrageously in public, the congressman looked to see Lincoln's reaction. Lincoln was undisturbed by the incident and explained to the incredulous congressman that such outbursts made his wife feel so much better that he hardly wanted to put a stop to them.

It seems likely that, at the time of the attack, Lincoln did not remain committed to his marriage because of attraction. He may have stayed because of obligation—a commitment to his own values. As a result, his wife's declaration of war could not disturb his commitment to an enduring union.

Was Lincoln trapped in a hopeless and unhealthy relationship? Not very likely. It's more probable that, like John Glenn, he sincerely loved his wife the way she was and was more interested in his commitment to the relationship, with all its long-term pleasures and demands, than he was in flawless personal happiness for himself at all times. Maybe he was committed to work steadily toward the harvest of healthy companionship.

The third kind of commitment is constraint. This can be called the "have to" kind of commitment. Some people stay in a relationship because of the children, because of social consequences of divorce, or because of financial limitations. Some stay in a relationship simply because getting out seems too scary or risky. This isn't the kind of commitment that can be expected to make a marriage flourish yet it can keep people in a relationship through a bad patch. Rather than give up on the garden during a dry spell, we persist. Extra effort is needed to keep the plants from wilting and dying, but normal weather returns and the garden flourishes again.

Linda Waite and colleagues found that "two out of three unhappily married adults who avoided divorce or separation ended up happily married five years later." She wrote that "one reason divorce is relatively high in our society is because now either person can leave, and we are more willing to leave than we used to be if we hit a bad patch. We're less likely to work it through. But there's evidence that dramatic turnarounds are commonplace. They're the typical experience."

Even commitment based on constraint can be good for marriage.

Reflection

How important is each kind of commitment to you?

+ Are you inclined to honor a relationship with commitment because of the attractions? What are you already doing to keep those attractions front-and-center in your mind?
+ Do you stay in a relationship because you believe that it is right to stay? Do you see it as a vow, obligation, or duty? If so, do you give yourself credit for the nobility of unselfish sacrifice?
+ Do you stay in a relationship because you see no good way of getting out? Are you willing to infuse new life into the relationship to see if it will flourish?
+ Do you tell your relationship story to yourself and others in ways that show two people working to appreciate each other and cultivate companionship? If so, you are cultivating commitment.

How Can We Cultivate Commitment?

What can we do to maintain and strengthen commitment in marriage? Here are a few ways to do it.

Make the Relationship Primary

With many demands on our time, sometimes our marriages only get cold leftovers from last night's dinner. Marriage may get only small fragments of spare time and energy. This is likely to leave the relationship starved and empty.

In contrast, when decisions are made about how we use our time and energy, the effect on the relationship should be considered. Does my hobby interfere with essential relationship time? Do my friends come before my spouse?

Make Couple Time a Priority

John Gottman, one of the world's leaders in marriage research, has observed that it is not the trips to Hawaii that ensure the strength of a relationship as much as the common, shared, regular activities. Some couples work in the yard together. Some cook together. Some attend church together.

Bill Doherty describes taking time every day to just talk with his wife Leah for a few minutes. Usually right after dinner they send the children to play while they share with each other. They do not use the time to solve relationship problems or to deal with conflicts. They use it to connect. This small commitment feeds the companionship.

30

Set Limits on Intrusions

For commitment to thrive, a couple must be willing to set some boundaries. For example, a couple could decide that they will not invite a member of the extended family to come live with them unless they have discussed it together and have come to agreement. Some couples agree not to talk with anyone outside the relationship about their marriage problems unless that person is a friend of the relationship—that is, someone who wants to help them succeed as a couple. Some couples decide that both partners will avoid going out to dinner or spending time alone with someone who could be a threat to the relationship. Some couples agree to carefully monitor their feelings of attraction to others outside the relationship so that they won't allow other attractions to grow.

Build Rituals of Connection

Each couple can design rituals of connection that can help sustain relationship commitment. Some couples take classes together and share their discoveries with each other. Some couples take time for hugging, walking, running, or other exercising. Any activity that helps a couple to feel close can strengthen and support commitment. For many couples it takes years to find the right activities that both partners enjoy. Even then, they require periodic readjustment.

Commit as a Positive Choice

Commitment in a relationship does not have to be left to chance. It can be a choice.

John Gottman has suggested things that couples can do to strengthen their relationship. They can keep a list—or scrapbook—of great moments in the relationship. Each partner can work to stay aware of qualities and strengths in the person he or she loves. When there are problems, rather than conclude that the relationship is a sinking ship, they can see the trouble as a passing storm.

Scott Stanley and his colleagues have described ways to cultivate commitment. They write,

> Most people seem to want a lifelong best friend in a mate. While for many couples this may come easily, the message for most couples is that it takes some work to nurture such a union. Constraint can lend stability, but it is dedication that can fuel a bonded, lifelong friendship. The good news is that the factors that underlie dedication are things about which people have choices. People can choose how they will handle the allure of alternatives. People can choose the priority they will place on their relationships. People can choose to nurture a positive, long-term vision for their relationship. And people can choose to think of commitment either as loss or gain.

One of the challenges we face in commitment is that we often try very hard but experience no improvement in our relationship. This can be discouraging. The problem may be that effective commitment includes working hard *and* working smart. When we are doing the wrong things, working harder at them won't help. Sometimes we must learn new ways.

One of the best ways to build commitment and to strengthen a relationship is to fill it with positives. Gottman suggests that the magic ratio is five positives for each negative. This ratio is the most important key to a healthy relationship. Later chapters in this book will give many more ideas for nurturing the potential of your relationship.

Commitment is more than a white-knuckled resolve to hold on through tough times. It includes the willingness and goodness to strengthen the relationship with positives.

Bearing Fruit over Time

Those who are committed to investing in their marriage are likely to enjoy a relationship that gets better and better over time. Although there are clearly relationships where two people are destroying each other and the relationship should end, most relationships would probably benefit from a little more commitment.

I have learned more about growth, struggle, pain, and misunderstanding from almost forty years of marriage with Nancy than I learned in all the rest of my life put together. I'm glad for those humbling and enlarging lessons.

I can also say I have learned more about joy, trust, happiness, unselfishness, peace, and purposeful living from Nancy than from all the people I have ever known. Maybe, as Thomas Paine suggested, we value the things that we have labored over. A single tomato from a cherished plant is cause for celebration. A simple breakthrough in marital understanding is cause for joy.

Daniel Wile, a wise therapist and writer, has observed that "there is value, when choosing a long-term partner, in realizing that you will inevitably be choosing a particular set of irresolvable problems that you'll be grappling with for the next ten, twenty, or fifty years." There is no perfect marriage. Every marriage has conflicts or problems, many of which will never be resolved.

In the absence of commitment, even the most promising plot of land bears no fruit. In the absence of commitment, even the most promising relationships will not grow. Commitment is not always fun. But we only get to strong relationships by struggling through storms, droughts, and pests. Yet the harvest can be glorious.

Exercise

Read over the following list of ways to show commitment; mark those that you or your spouse already do well. You might also mark those that you would like to learn to do well.

	Things I Already Do Well	Things I Would Like to Do Better	Things My Partner Already Does Well
I make time to do things with my spouse.			
I try to honor occasions that are important to my spouse (anniversaries and so on).			
I don't flirt with anyone except my spouse.			
I have worked with my spouse to establish traditions that bring us close.			
When I promise my spouse that I will do something, I do it.			
I put effort into making our time together special.			
I look for and remember the good qualities in my partner.			
I make a point of remembering our good times.			
I keep confidences.			
I don't share details of my intimate relationship with anyone outside the relationship.			
I speak kindly of my spouse in private and in public.			
I don't speak poorly of my spouse to others.			

Chapter 2

Grow

It Takes Vibrant People to Create Vibrant Relationships

Having a healthy marriage is more than finding the right person,
it's becoming the right person.

—LOLLY PISONI

Coauthor Wally and his wife, Nancy, had an eighty-five-year-old neighbor named Elizabeth who always kept her garden tidy and abundant. She was an absolute delight. A midlife immigrant from Scotland, she was lively, funny, and energetic. To stay healthy she ran laps within her small house. She also did strength exercises. She had a witty and lively mind that never ceased to grow, right along with her garden.

Wearing an old house dress, Elizabeth worked in her garden daily and gathered up the dust in the alleyway to use as fill dirt in her yard. When her St. Augustine grass started to grow over the sidewalk, she clipped it and replanted it elsewhere in her yard. She loved to grow impatiens, irises, roses, and English ivy. Though most of her contemporaries had departed for the garden in the sky, Elizabeth kept her garden vibrant because of her personal vitality.

The same principle applies to cultivating our marriages. People who are vibrant and flourishing bring much more to their marriages. Those who are morose and dreary, whose lives are drained of purpose, are likely to find their marriages wilting as well.

So, right after talking about commitment and before diving into the stuff you expect in a marriage book, we want to talk with you about being a healthy, vibrant, flourishing human being.

Improving Our Well-Being

Over the years, psychology and medicine have prescribed many ways of improving our well-being. Some of these are well known. We all know that we should exercise regularly. We know that we should eat lots of fresh fruits and vegetables. We know we should get adequate amounts of sleep. Some authorities recommend meditation. Others recommend continuing education, workshops, trainings, travel, reading for pleasure, inspiration, and knowledge.

In this chapter, we want to focus on how to flourish psychologically. You may (or may not) know that there has been a revolution in psychology since about 1999. Before that time, the field had become quite focused on treating and curing mental illness but had neglected mental wellness. We could describe myriad ways of being mentally troubled but had scant counsel for those who wanted to flourish.

The popular assumption seemed to be that, if you can get rid of the sickness, everything else will take care of itself. This doesn't make sense. It is like saying that, if you got the weeds and bugs out of the garden, the garden would flourish without any additional care. The truth is that gardens still require light, water, and maintenance.

Since 1999, many of the world's best psychologists have dedicated thousands of hours to discovering and describing how we can flourish. What does it take to be a vibrant, happy human? What are the keys to well-being? At the end of this chapter we list some of the best resources for learning about well-being. Now we want to summarize some of the great discoveries that make you happier. We want to help you be as energetic and vibrant as our friend Elizabeth.*

Authentic Happiness

One of my favorite happy-cologists is Martin Seligman. He has been a leader in the new positive psychology movement and has described what years of research say about how to be truly happy. The kind of happiness Seligman describes is not the fleeting hiccup of giddiness that comes from a good laugh but the steady, enduring stuff that makes life meaningful. He calls this authentic happiness.

There's something interesting about Seligman and his discoveries. He is not Mr. Giggles, spouting feel-good advice. He is a serious scientist who only believes an idea when good research commands his respect. Yet his suggestions sound like the kind of things you might have heard from a wise grandparent or an earnest Sunday school teacher. Of course, when research and

---

* Elizabeth has since died—at the age of eighty-seven—but she lived vibrantly until the end. We miss her.

common sense agree, maybe we have found some truths that will endure!

Seligman recommends three things: savoring, flow, and service. The balance of this chapter will talk about how to have more of these happiness-bearing activities in your life. As your life feels more and more meaningful, you are likely to find that your marriage gets even better at the same time.

Savoring

Happiness is a process, not a destination.
—UNKNOWN

Savoring involves relishing, enjoying, delighting in, and appreciating. Pause right now. What can you savor right this minute? Do you see pictures of loved ones nearby? Are you in a comfortable chair? Do you have a favorite keepsake nearby? Do you hear sounds that you enjoy? Can you smell dinner cooking? Do you have a piece of fresh fruit awaiting you?

Much of the time our minds run on autopilot. We don't notice the thousands of things happening around us. Maybe we fret about the mistakes of the past and worry about challenges in the future. Alarm bells are constantly ringing in our heads. Our minds are filled with troubles even as we are surrounded by opportunities.

The passionate novelist Thomas Clayton Wolfe described the common experience of humans: "Poor, dismal, ugly, sterile, shabby little man . . . with your scrabble of harsh oaths. . . . Joy, glory, and magnificence were here for you . . . but you scrabbled along . . . rattling a few stale words . . . and would have none of them" (quoted in Peters). Most of us are like commuters passing through grand scenery but so absorbed in reading a newspaper that we might as well be shivering under a bridge.

Seligman talks about three kinds of savoring. He says that we can savor the present, the past, and the future. Let's start with the present.

Savoring the Present

How do we become better savorers? How do we learn to tune in to the goodness that surrounds us?

Savoring is a choice. It is a choice to notice and appreciate our worlds and our lives. I have a friend named Dave who likes to ask people this question: When was the last time you felt joy? What would you say if Dave asked you? Would you have to go back to a trip to Disneyland when you were nine years old? If you have to go back decades to identify an experience drenched with joy, maybe you need to practice savoring. Even if you can recall a joy experience within the last week, maybe you can still enlarge your capacity to savor life and find joy.

If Dave asked me that question today, I would say: "A few minutes ago a colleague and I were playing with a toy—a plastic hemisphere that, when turned inside out and placed on a counter, will jump in the air. We laughed. Before that I called Nancy on the phone and talked about her day. She told me excitedly about getting new orthotics at a discounted price. Very little is needed to lead a happy life! Earlier I joked with a couple of friends. One of them advised, 'Have fun and eat chocolate.' We chuckled. Life felt full and rich. My day is filled with joy!"

It is also true that those joy experiences have been interspersed with tiredness, boredom, and a dread of choosing exactly the right words for these sentences. Yet, as soon as I began to write, the fog lifted. When I looked at my colleagues and enjoyed their personalities, my spirits climbed. Every time I call Nancy, I know I will enjoy her kindness and gentle laughter. I will enjoy Nancy not only because she is a truly beautiful human being, but also because I *choose* to notice and enjoy her kindness and sweetness. All of this is savoring.

Some people have a knack for savoring every moment and blessing of life. I remember an older man who told me one Sunday morning how grateful he was for the ability to see, for running water in his kitchen and food in the pantry, and for sweet companionship in his life. My reaction was immediate. I take a lot for granted! I am also grateful for sight, running water, food, and companionship—but I can't remember the last time I was consciously grateful for any of those great blessings. I routinely fail to notice the good things in life.

James once had a friend named George who said he had given a lot of thought to the question, "How are you doing?" He said he wasn't satisfied with the standard answers that he, and most other folks he knew, gave. He was tired of saying and hearing things like "Fine," "Good," "OK," and "All right." He knew there had to be more.

One day George was having a particularly good day (he may have discovered three scoops of raisins in his Raisin Bran) when someone asked him that oft-repeated question. Without thinking, he responded, "It's my best day so far." That was it! He had found the perfect answer to the question "How are you doing?"

George has been answering that question the same way for years now. But one might wonder, could it be true that every day since he first uttered those words has been better than the one before? I suspect not. In fact, I'm positive that some days have seemed especially tough. However, his choosing to respond with "It's my best day so far" has been a constant reminder to George to savor—to pay attention to all the things he has to be grateful for every day.

Do we enjoy the sun on our faces, the wonderful variety of foods available to us, a roof overhead, and people to love? Many people assume they can't have more fun unless they have more money. Research shows that, if we are not going hungry, having more money will not make us significantly happier. The key to happiness is appreciating the blessings we already have.

One of my favorite models of savoring is provided by Emily's soliloquy from the play *Our Town*, by Thornton Wilder. As she turns back the clock and returns to her life as a twelve-year-old, the ordinary seems truly extraordinary: the people she loved, the ticking of clocks, her mother's sunflowers, food, dresses, and baths. Somehow it was just all too amazing when seen through fresh eyes. Every minute was a blessing and miracle. Emily wonders, "Do any human beings ever realize life while they live it—every, every minute?"

The narrator of the play tells Emily that the only ones who even occasionally enjoy life are the saints and poets. We can join that grateful group as we learn to savor.

Reflection

Take a few minutes to respond to these questions:

+ What have you enjoyed just today that you can now reflect on and savor? You may want to close your eyes and go back through your day. Maybe you will want to make a note of some of the tender mercies of life that you can savor.

+ What can you do to notice and enjoy the blessings of life as they arise?

Savoring the Past

Seligman observes that in addition to savoring the present moment, we can also savor our pasts. This is in stark contrast to our usual ways of thinking. It is quite natural to treasure our resentments and disappointments. We may remember the people who misjudged or mistreated us. Or we may stockpile recollections of our own blunders. Neither of those is savoring. Both of them drain us of energy and hope.

We humans have a serious problem with our usual way of processing our pasts. We sometimes think of our memories as a faithful recording of experiences. We believe that we remember exactly what happened. What we generally fail to recognize is that our recollections of the past are much like the stories children tell about their doings.

For example, a little boy may say that he was sitting on the playground building a castle in the sand when a monster exploded from the ground and knocked over his sister's sand castle. We suspect that his story may not be a faithful description of precisely what happened.

Children's stories are filled with imagination, selective perception, and what we might call "creativity in the service of exoneration." The same is true of adults. That is why, when we share stories at family gatherings, a family member will object: "That's not how it happened!" An argument will ensue with each person thinking he or she has the truth and the other has either a bad memory or a problem with honesty.

Research now tells us that we compact memories when we save them. Every time we open an old memory, we try to restore detail but inevitably add new detail or subtract old detail. Without realizing it, we even color the facts to shape the story to our liking. Maybe we want to make Aunt Nellie into a bully and Uncle Fred into a hapless and good-hearted victim. Every time we retell the story to ourselves or others, we refine the story to fit our purposes. You can see how this process can lead to a story that is vastly different from other people's recollections.

This process can work negatively or positively. We can tell our stories in ways that make us into helpless victims. We can create a life story filled with loss and loneliness. Or we can distill the lessons and blessings from our experiences and tell a story of the same life filled with purpose and growth. We get to choose the themes of our stories by the details we emphasize and the slant we bring to the stories. It is a choice.

You can see how this relates to savoring our pasts. We can choose to inventory all those times that people hurt and cheated us. Or we can celebrate the good people and blessed experiences that overflow our histories. They are there. They may have quiet voices and small parts—but they are there in even the most troubled lives. We will find them if we go looking for them.

This is not to say that all the goodness we find in our lives is an invention. There is goodness in every life. It can be written out of our stories or it can be featured. And, even in those cases where goodness seems to be intermixed with lots of badness, we can distill out the good. We can look for the best in people and honor that part of their actions that was noble.

As I examine my life for examples of goodness, I think of my fifth-grade teacher, Rhea Bailey, who was a warm and loving presence in my life. I think of Ray Gilbert, my high school trig teacher, who inspired me to be kind and to love life. I'm reminded of Phil Ellis, an administrator in the school system where I first taught, who made me think I could do something creative with my life.

Closer to home, I can remember the great times that my brother, Alan, and I had. Or I can recollect our scuffles. I can remember the time Mom was mad at me for teasing my sister, or I can remember the time she carried me to a shrub and held me up to look into a bird's nest and see three perfect robin's eggs. I can remember the time Dad lectured me about responsibility or the time he built me a fort out of bales of hay.

If I gather up and cherish the finest moments, my life will feel rich and blessed. That is savoring the past. Can you think of sweet moments of delight in your family life?

Seligman recommends one predictably joyous way of savoring our pasts: we can all write gratitude letters. We think of someone who has blessed us, and we write a letter describing what that person did and expressing our gratitude. He suggests that we deliver the letter personally and read it to the person if that is possible.

Though my father has been gone for ten years, I have written a letter to my mother, who is still well, thank goodness, expressing my gratitude for lifting me to look into that nest—and for lifting me to see wonder and goodness all through my life. I have even written a letter to my great-grandfather, who died years before I was born but whose journal, filled with stories of serving the people of New Zealand as a Christian missionary, was given to me.

He and his journal have blessed my life immeasurably. Though I could not find an easy way to deliver a letter to my long-gone ancestor, I was blessed by writing it.

Reflection

Take a few minutes to respond to this question:

- Who are the people who have blessed and enriched your life? (They may have also hurt you at times. But add them to your list if they somehow blessed and enriched your life.) You might like to write about the ways they blessed your life. You might like to write them a letter—even if you cannot deliver it. Try savoring your past and finding those gems that have enriched your life story.

Savoring the Future

It is easy to see how we can savor the present and the past. It may be less obvious how we can savor the future. Let's begin by considering how we instinctively think about the future. Many of us fret: What if my job is eliminated? What if our car breaks down? What if one of the children is hurt or abducted? What if I am disabled? There are almost limitless opportunities for fretting!

It is a good thing that the human mind is trained to see danger; it often prevents us from getting hurt. Centuries ago, for example, it made sense to worry about lions, bears, and snakes. Being alert to danger might make the difference between living a productive life and becoming a predator's lunch.

But times have changed. Most of us do not face serious threats from wild animals. Unfortunately, we still have the same tendency to react very strongly to perceived threats. When a spouse says something unkind or when someone cuts us off in traffic, we may go almost crazy with rage.

Today more people are killed by anxiety and worry than by wild animals. Living in fear damages our hearts and may cause us to overreact to small challenges. It is better for our well-being that we stay mindful of good things in our past and present while looking forward with hope to the future.

Many of us allow our gentle, tender, positive emotions to be swamped by our brutal self-preservation instincts. If we want to thrive in marriage, we need to learn to listen more to our gentle emotions and less to our savage self-protective emotions. Rather than see our spouses as threatening lions, bears, or snakes determined to kill us, we can see them as good people who are trying to raise a healthy garden with us. Rather than live in fear and dread, imagining every kind of unhappiness and misery, we can be optimistic. We can look forward to new challenges as opportunities for learning and growth. We can turn stumbling blocks into a beautiful garden path.

If we don't manage anxiety, it will fill our lives with relentless dread. In his book *Science of Fear*, Daniel Gardner suggests that our natural anxiety together with media fear-mongering lead us to be unrealistically anxious. He suggests that we change our way of thinking: "Whatever challenges we face, it remains indisputably true that those living in the developed world are the safest, healthiest and richest humans who ever lived." Most of the things we worry about will never be a problem. We can deal sensibly with challenges when they do arrive rather than borrowing pain from an imagined future.

So, how do we savor the future? There are many ways! We can train ourselves to look forward to the blessings ahead. We look forward to the flowers that bloom in spring. We plan the trip we will have this summer. We await the bounty at the farmer's market when fall arrives. We anticipate the fun and friendship that come with the holiday season. We can train our minds to look to the future with joyful anticipation rather than white-knuckle dread. This savoring of the future is even more helpful when we regularly anticipate little things every day and every week.

One of Seligman's discoveries is that those people who tend to think mostly about the good things in their lives are the happiest. They may not be very objective. In fact, they may exaggerate and embellish the good. And that is good for human growth! When we have a choice between seeing the wilted flowers or the new growth in our lives, why not look for the new growth?

Reflection

Take a few minutes to respond to these questions:

- What do you look forward to this evening? Will you be eating a favorite food? Will you be doing something satisfying with your spouse? Are you taking a class or workshop? Will you be returning to a favorite book? What good things are likely to happen to you just today? This week? This month? This year?

• When anxiety arises, how can you deal with it in a balanced and positive way? What are your sources of hope?

Moving from Savoring to Flow

So far we have talked about three kinds of savoring that can improve the quality of our lives. After savoring, Seligman recommends flow. Flow is any time we use our talents in a challenging task and get so absorbed that we lose track of time. In other words, when we design our lives to use our talents regularly, life is better.

Flow is not about fun and recreation. It is about creation. It is about using our talents or strengths in challenging tasks. It may surprise you to know that people tend to have more flow at work than in their leisure time. That does not mean that work is inherently more satisfying than home life. It probably means that we sometimes shove our lives into neutral and coast through our non-working hours. The more promising course is to take on projects that fit our talents and yet challenge us.

My dear Nancy likes to visit lonely people. She is energized by visiting them! She comes home from such visits just glowing.

I love woodworking. I am always dreaming up some excuse to buy lumber and start building. When a project is complete, I call the neighbors over to pat me on the back.

James's wife, Kathie, loves quilting. The fabric is her canvas. She has a knack for choosing fabrics that look great together and piecing them together into works of art. James does "cartwheels" every time she completes a quilt.

You may love singing, jogging, reading, writing, carving, scrapbooking, cooking—there are so many ways to express ourselves! When we design our lives to allow us to use our talents in challenging tasks, our lives are enriched.

I remember when Hurricane Opal hit our house in Auburn, Alabama, and turned our neighborhood into a war zone. We were without power and phone for two weeks and were overwhelmed by the daunting task of removing fallen trees from our yard and putting our lives back together. (I gladly recognize that our challenges were small compared to some that others have suffered.) I found myself growing weary and disinterested in life. When I finally realized that I was depressed, I sat down to figure out what I needed to do. The biggest surprise that came from that reflection was that I needed to be doing some of the things that I love to do! I needed to make time for hobbies or reading favorite books. I had set aside all my hobbies and focused on the challenges of repairing our home. I think my soul was telling me that it needed to be reenergized with tasks that I love to do.

That was a particular surprise because it didn't seem that adding one more job to an overloaded life was any kind of solution. But it was. As I made a little time to plan and build a suspended track for my childhood Lionel train, I had more energy for dealing with fallen trees and a damaged house.

Reflection

Think of times when you have gotten so absorbed in a challenging task that you lost track of time. It could be any number of things: singing, learning, jogging, offering compassion, cooking, sewing, woodworking, and so on. What were you doing?

Identifying Strengths

To have flow, we must know and use our strengths. Some think in terms of traditional talents such as music and dance. There are also personal or personality talents. Some people have taken personality tests like the Myers-Briggs Type Indicator. Such tests (available through counselors as well as online) can help us know our personal strengths.

Seligman has developed a different way of assessing talents: character strengths. By taking the VIA Signature Strengths Survey, you can find out what strengths you have—such as creativity, loyalty, humility, fairness, and kindness. He has identified twenty-four such qualities of character. Seligman calls each person's top five strengths *signature strengths*.

Maybe Eric Liddell, the Olympic runner, was describing flow when he said, "I believe God made me for a purpose, but he also made me fast. And when I run I feel His pleasure." Liddell is describing that sense of *everything-is-right* that accompanies using our talents. Pay attention to the times when you experience this feeling.

Reflection

Take a few minutes to respond to these questions:

• What do you already know about your talents or strengths?
• Are there some tests you are interested in taking to learn more about your talents? (For more information about

52

these tests, see the resource list at the end of this book.)

- What work—paid or unpaid—have you most enjoyed doing? How can you adjust your life to do more of what you love to do?
- What things does your spouse love to do? How can you support him or her in those activities?
- What tasks do you and your spouse love to do together? How can you make space in your life for those things you both enjoy?

Serving

So far we have discussed the first two of Seligman's recommendations for greater well-being—savoring and flow. The third key to well-being is serving. Each of us can dedicate some part of our lives to making our world a better place. For example, Nancy and I have a dear friend who is a single mother of four children. She almost always feels overwhelmed. We have volunteered to help her any way we can. She sometimes invites us to help her with household repairs and care for her children. Sometimes we take her and the children out for dinner. About once a week we have them over to our house for dinner and games. She says that our efforts are a real blessing to her. They are also a blessing for us. Our lives are enriched by our love and involvement with them.

Seligman is right. When we serve other people, we are happier and our lives are more meaningful. Some of the service we do we may do without our spouses. For example, I sometimes mentor students in physics and math—subjects in which Nancy has little interest. But we also find ways that we can serve together as in helping the single mother described above. This principle of service is so important that an entire chapter is dedicated to discussing it (see Chapter Six).

There are many ways to serve! Whether we are good at offering a listening ear, teaching, caring for the environment, organizing—whatever it is—our lives are better when we dedicate some part of our time to service.

Reflection

Take a few minutes to respond to these questions:

• What are some ways you have enjoyed serving in the past? Do you currently have projects that allow you to give back? What adjustments would you like to make to give service a prominent place in your life? Are there ways that you and your partner like to serve together?
• How would you like to design your life in order to more effectively savor, flow, and serve?

You can easily see the application of these principles to marriage. A partner who is bored and stale is not as likely to have a great marriage as the partner who is vibrant and flourishing.

When two people are vibrant and growing, they have more to bring to their marriage. Of course, if either partner gets so wrapped up in personal development that he or she makes no investment in the partnership, the relationship is damaged.

Growing requires balance. Both partners work to be vibrant, happy individuals. Yet they also make sure that their personal development does not get in the way of their partnership.

Reflection

Take a few minutes to respond to these questions:

- What are some activities, hobbies, and interests that help you stay vibrant? What are some of the activities and interests that help your spouse stay vibrant?
- How can you support each other in your individual growth and well-being?

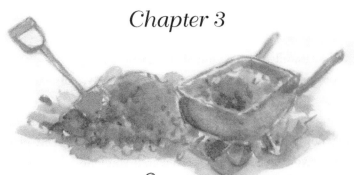

Chapter 3

Nurture

Do the Work of Loving

Kindness consists of loving people more than they deserve.
—JOSEPH JOUBERT

Great gardens have a unique ability to inspire us. At their best, they are magical places that transport us from a world of chaos and noise to a world of beauty and peace.

The loveliest gardens look quite natural. They appear as if they happened without effort. Yet, even if we have done very little gardening ourselves, we suspect that wise and sustained effort was necessary to create the magical place. The gardeners do not merely back up a truck once a year and dump several tons of fertilizer in the hopes that the garden will then flourish. No. Good gardeners do several things consistently:

+ Watch for and deal with bugs and blights
+ Water according to the needs of the plants
+ Prune plants to ensure optimal growth

- Add carefully planned nutrients to the soil
- Continue to add new plants to enrich the environment

In other words, a glorious garden is not an accident. If you merely dump tons of fertilizer, you will probably kill many plants and waste your investment in fertilizer. If you ignore bugs and pests, your garden may be destroyed.

Nurturing a relationship means to care for, look after, and provide those conditions that will make your marriage flourish. But the effort necessary to sustain a healthy garden is different in Arkansas than it is in Michigan, California, or Arizona. Experienced gardeners know that no one fertilizer is good for every part of every garden or every part of the country. We must study the nature of the soil and the needs of the particular plants that we have. One garden—or one area of the garden—may need more compost stirred in. Another area may need lime. To randomly throw even the best of fertilizers into the garden without first assessing the specific needs of the soil and the plants almost guarantees that more harm than good will come of your efforts.

The same is true in marriage. Different people need different emotional nutrients in order to feel that they are loved.

Growing into Marriage

Let's look at our own human development for a minute. When we were first born, we may have been cute (this can be debated), but we were definitely not considerate. A newborn does not come out of the birth canal saying, "Wow! I can see that all of you have been through a lot. Why don't you set me aside for a few hours and I'll chill while all of you get a good rest." Nope. A newborn comes out demanding constant attention. Even through the first months of life this doesn't change very much. When a baby is hungry or uncomfortable, he or she will torture you with a piercing cry until you attend to his or her needs.

This is all very understandable. Babies cannot care for themselves. They need our care. Even when children are a few years old, we often expect them to be considerate and to share their toys with other children long before they are developmentally ready to do so. (In my experience, children can probably share with other children when they are about six years old, have plenty of toys for themselves, like the children they are playing with, and are in good moods.)

Human development continues. By the time we are teens, we should understand that other people have different preferences, and we can start to honor those preferences. We finally understand that, for example, just because I love tapioca pudding, this doesn't mean that everyone should. I become capable of seeing the world through other people's eyes. Of course it is also common for us to start dividing into cliques. We often decide that our style, neighborhood, religion, or preferences are better than those of other people. Sometimes we divide the world into two main groups: us and them. "Us" includes the people we like and agree with. "Them" includes anyone else (in other words, people we don't like or agree with). We may move people out of our group and into "them" when they irritate us.

Somewhere in early adulthood, most of us marry. We drag into this hopeful relationship a whole lot of baggage from our human development. Like little children, we still want to fuss when we are uncomfortable; we want someone to make it right. We want to be taken care of.

We still have trouble sharing. We don't want other people spending our money and using our toys. And yet marriage demands lots and lots of sharing! With our partners we share our time, our income, our living space, and even our bodies.

When our partners start to irritate us, we begin to wonder if we married one of "them." We wonder if our spouses have changed or have hidden their true natures from us. We thought we married an "us" but find ourselves living with a "them."

Can We Be Less Self-Centered?

There are two plausible conclusions: (1) People were not designed for the challenges of marriage. (2) Marriage challenges us to keep growing from our self-centered beginnings toward an ability to cooperate and share with another human being.

Sometimes the first conclusion seems most persuasive. It just seems too hard to surrender our own ways in order to be with another person. It seems almost impossible! And when almost half of once-jubilant marriages end in painful divorce and untold others suffer from coldness and distance, there is reason to suspect that humans were not designed for long-term relationships.

Yet the second conclusion should be seriously considered. Just as we were challenged by wise and loving parents to move from the self-centeredness of infancy and through the fickleness of adolescence, marriage now challenges and invites us to learn advanced lessons in humanity. We are being invited to learn how to see another person's point of view, to have compassion for our partners' pains, to share our time and resources with another person. Marriage might be, as clergyman Joseph Barth has suggested, "our last, best chance to grow up." If he is right, then we should expect marriage to stretch us, challenges us, frustrate us, and eventually enlarge us.

Maybe we struggle with marriage because nobody ever told us that it was supposed to stretch us. Maybe we enter marriage expecting sweet companionship and feel like throwing a tantrum when we discover that it is yet another opportunity to grow—an opportunity to expand ourselves and to become more patient and compassionate. As people prepare for marriage, we often encourage them to find the right person and rarely teach them how to be the right person—someone who values others and can look beyond their own immediate self-interest.

Some scholars have suggested that many people today cannot, as Roy Baumeister writes, "really accept the possibility that a good, loving relationship could entail genuine costs and sacrifices to the self. . . . The new attitude is that if a relationship is detrimental to the self, then it *should* be terminated. A stale or stultifying or oppressive marriage should not continue. The person has a right, even an obligation to move on."

If, however, marriage is designed to help us grow up, then moving on from our current marriage is like dropping out of one school after another. Therefore, the best solution for those normal marriages that have many strengths, may be some tutoring to improve our functioning in the present school rather than quitting and hoping to find an easier curriculum elsewhere. Or, to return to the gardening metaphor, rather than selling a house when the garden starts languishing, maybe we can learn to be better gardeners.

A Sign of Maturity

The clearest evidence that we have grown up is when we do perspective taking—when we are able to understand and appreciate another person's point of view.

I remember when Nancy and I went with another couple to a community lecture. After it was over, I asked the couple how they

61

liked the lecture. The rather deliberate husband said, "Well. I liked it. But the guy sure did talk fast." The wife reacted: "No he didn't. It was just right." They fussed with each other for several minutes about the speed of the lecture. So we ask, which of them was right?

Maybe you can see the answer coming: Both were right. The husband liked to have more time to think about ideas. He prefers a slower pace of delivery. The wife wasn't bothered by the pace. She enjoyed the lecture. And maybe she thought it impolite for her husband to criticize the lecturer. (It is worth noting that she didn't seem to think it was impolite to criticize her husband.)

Let's suggest how they might do a little perspective taking. After the husband had staked out his initial preference, his wife might have said: "You like more time to think about things, don't you, dear? I enjoyed the lecture a lot, but I can see that it was delivered too fast to have time to reflect on the ideas." Her statement honors his preference while still stating her own.

Let's suppose that the wife had already spit out her comment. How could the husband take his wife's point of view? He might have said, "You're so right, dear. I am a tortoise. I like time to think about ideas. And you are a quick thinker. I'm glad the lecture was just right for you."

Of course most of us hate to pass up an opportunity to take offense or feel insulted. It is not easy or natural for us to get outside of our own perspectives—which is why it is such a remarkable accomplishment. Rare as it is, it also makes a big difference in the quality of our relationships.

Seeing Our Partners' Points of View

Seeing our partners' points of view is essential to nurturing our relationships. How can we respond lovingly to our partners' needs and preferences when we don't know their needs and preferences? We must get outside of our own views and into our partners' views if we hope to nurture a vibrant relationship. Let's consider another example.

One Monday morning a coworker told me that he had celebrated his wedding anniversary over the weekend. I asked him how it went. He sighed. He told me that he had wanted to do something very special for his wife. So he arranged for one of his wife's girlfriends to take her shopping on the day of their anniversary. In his wife's absence, he snuck home from work and prepared a sumptuous meal, put out candles and the best china. When his wife came home from shopping, he was ready with his big surprise.

When his wife came into the house and found a lovely meal and beautiful table, she was surprised. "Wow. Thank you, dear." Pause. "That was very thoughtful of you."

Her enthusiasm was less than the husband expected, so he inquired. "What's wrong, dear? Did I do something wrong?"

"No, no!" was her quick reply. "This is very kind of you. Thank you, dear."

He wasn't convinced. "Tell me what's wrong."

She was reluctant. After some urging she said, "Sweetheart, you work long hours. You're gone a lot. If you're going to take a day off from work, don't send me shopping! I want to spend the day with you."

My colleague had made a real sacrifice to show his love to his wife. Unfortunately it was not the sacrifice she preferred. Sometimes less is more—especially when it is the right thing. If he had taken off even an hour or two from work and spent it with her, she would have appreciated it more than a luscious meal in which he invested a whole day without her.

Sending Messages of Love

Imagine that one afternoon your partner suddenly grabs you for no apparent reason, gazes into your eyes, and declares: "I love you with all my heart!" What would your reaction be?

Depending on your personality, you might be thrilled. You might wish that your partner would express himself or herself this way more often! However, this sudden display of affection might make you wonder if your spouse had wrecked the car. Or maybe you suspect he's drunk. Or maybe you think she wants to get you in the mood to spend some money.

Consider a different example. Imagine that your spouse leaves you a beautifully wrapped box. You open it to find an expensive ring. What would your reaction be?

Again, it's possible that you might be ecstatic—you could feel you have the world's most thoughtful husband. But depending on your personality, you may wonder how you're going to pay for it. Or you may wonder why he didn't buy a different one. Or you could wish he had bought you a puppy, a new computer, or new furniture.

Gardens Can Wilt

When we first began our relationships with the people we later married, we were filled with warmth, love, and enthusiasm. It all seemed so natural. Nearly every expression of love seemed absolutely perfect.

But those feelings of romance only last so long. Within two years, most couples have returned to earth. It may then seem like irritation is more common than closeness. The demands of daily living deplete our marital soil of vital nutrients. Our garden wilts. We now have to put effort into figuring out what our partners really want so that our love can continue to thrive.

I (Wally) learned this lesson the hard way—by doing it wrong for many years. May I share my struggle to learn to effectively express my love to my dear Nancy?

I love stuff. I love it in virtually all forms. I love wind-up toys, scraps of wood, beautiful pictures, and picture frames. I love birds' eggs and ficus trees. I love stuff.

I feel loved when people give me stuff. And when I have wanted to show my love to Nancy, I have bought her stuff. I have often felt very proud of all the stuff I got her. But Nancy doesn't like stuff! When I have given her stuff, she has sometimes said, "Well, thanks, dear. I appreciate it. But I don't need it."

I would laugh. "You may not need it, but you can store it with all my stuff and be happy knowing that you have it."

Nancy wasn't convinced. She would grimace and say, "But we can't afford the stuff you bought me."

Again I would laugh. "That's not our problem. It's the bank's problem!"

Obviously Nancy and I had different ways of giving and receiving love. We had vastly different *love languages*.

Reviving Our Garden

When I asked Nancy what she wanted for her birthday, Christmas, or anniversary, her answer was always the same: "Nothing." I figured she was just being agreeable. For years I tried to spy on her. I tried to notice what she looked at when she was at a department store. But the stuff I bought her didn't please her. In fact she sometimes asked why I had bought it for her. I would say, "Because I saw you admiring it." She would respond, "Honey, I wasn't admiring it. I was wondering why anyone in the world would buy it." She continued to insist that she didn't want any stuff. I just couldn't imagine that! (I was stuck in my own view of the world.)

In the early days of our marriage, Nancy would write sweet notes to me and sneak them into my lunch box or my briefcase. When I found the notes, I was always pleased. But I also wondered why she didn't include any stuff.

Nancy is much more aware than I am. Even though she didn't care for stuff, she knew that I did. So she bought me stuff. Because she is frugal, it was often inexpensive stuff. It might be a little toy that was on sale. But it was stuff and I was happy.

After twenty-seven years of marriage and no success at figuring out what to get her for special occasions, I finally decided to try something different. I tried to notice the way she seemed to like receiving love. I noticed that she loved getting notes from me and from our children. She had often written me notes. Apparently Nancy's language of love was notes.

As Christmas approached I decided I should try writing her a note. So I pulled out my appointment book from the previous year. It reminded me of the places we had been and the things we had done. I worked my way through it looking for special experiences we had shared in the course of the previous year.

It took hours to go through the events of the year, but I ended up with a letter that was about four or five pages long telling about sweet experiences we had enjoyed in the months previous. I printed the letter on nice paper, decorated it with expensive stickers, put it in an envelope, and placed it under the Christmas tree.

As Christmas got closer, I started to panic. What if Nancy got mad because I didn't get her any stuff? What if the holiday felt flat for her because she didn't get what she wanted? But I didn't know what else to get her. So I decided to stick with the letter.

On Christmas morning our daughter, Sara, handed out presents. Nancy was perplexed to get an envelope. She opened it and began to read. As she read about our shared joys during the year, the tears began to trickle down her cheeks. As she finished the letter she turned to me and said, "Honey, this is what I always wanted for Christmas."

I replied, "Yes, but there will be some great sales after Christmas!"

It took twenty-seven years for me to figure out that Nancy wanted something very different from what I had been giving her. She wanted words of love and appreciation. Finally I had learned her language of love.

I suppose that the key to discovering Nancy's language of love was noticing how she preferred to show love. I could also have asked her how she liked to be loved. I could have noticed the loving gestures that had touched her heart in the past. Now I regularly give Nancy letters. It is a real sacrifice for me to take the time to gather information and write about the key events of our lives. But finally I have learned to express love in the way Nancy likes to receive it.

Reflection

Take a few minutes to respond to these questions:

- When have you seen the world from your partner's point of view? Did it help you to feel loving and appreciative toward your partner?
- If you showed love to your partner in the way she or he prefers, how would it affect your relationship?

How to Use Your Own Language of Love

One way of thinking about languages of love is that there are three specific languages.

- Show me
- Tell me
- Touch me

Show-me's value action. They don't want you to tell them you love them. They want specific acts. They may prefer a changed light bulb or Chinese takeout over words of endearment. For them, talk is cheap.

There are also tell-me's. They prefer to hear the words. Or they may like to see them written in letters or cards. They may want you to whisper words of love every day. Of course many tell-me's marry the strong, silent types who would rather be dragged down a country road than speak the obvious: "I told you I loved you when I married you. If it changes, I'll let you know."

Touch-me's like to be held or cuddled. Snuggling may be their favorite activity. They may or may not like lovemaking, but they definitely want to sit close and have their hands held. I have been surprised to find that this preference is at least as common among men as among women.

We can figure out how our spouses like to be loved by noticing what they enjoy and by talking about times they have felt loved.

With the following table, consider the meaning of each of the three languages and whether it describes the way you and your spouse like to be loved.

Languages of Love

	Show Me	Tell Me	Touch Me
	I like it when you show your love by helping me with tasks or by giving me things.	I like it when you express your love in words—either spoken or written.	I like to hold hands, cuddle, sit close, and be together.
How do you like to be loved? Mark your first, second, and third choices.			
How do you think your partner likes to be loved? Mark his or her first, second, and third choices.			

Exercises

After filling in the table:

* Think of times when your partner has loved you in a way that was very meaningful to you. What did your spouse do that you appreciated? Make a list of some of these experiences.

When you have each had a chance to list some experiences, go to the next exercise.

* Take turns sharing with your spouse your first, second, and third choices for languages of love. Tell about some of the times that you have felt loved and close. Pay special attention to stories told by your spouse. You can learn a lot about what matters to her or him.

Two More Ways to Love

Although there are usually some specific and unique ways in which each person likes to be loved, there are also two other languages of love that are important to most people. They are

* Spending time together
* Feeling understood

Just as gardens require regular attention, relationships require regular, enjoyable time together. Yet most of us fail to do this. What keeps us from doing it?

Sometimes our lives are very busy, and we can't find time to do things together. Sometimes we have a hard time agreeing on what to do together. Sometimes we have very little energy at the end of our busy days and weeks to do things together. Sometimes we can't afford the things we like to do.

How can we make time for our relationships? There are no genies in the lamp to solve this problem. Patience and creativity are required. One way to do this is to brainstorm three lists of activities you might like to participate in together. The first list should be simple activities that are free or relatively inexpensive. The second list might include moderately priced activities. The final list could include more expensive activities (for example, a vacation). With these lists, you will be prepared with ideas for fun activities no matter how much time you have or what your circumstances might be. Each partner might also make a list of things he or she enjoys, then work together to find agreed-on activities and times to do them.

There is a surprise about spending time together. We often think of things like a trip to Hawaii or at least dinner at a lovely restaurant as the kind of things we want to do together. The good news is that we can strengthen our relationship just as much by stirring up some homemade salsa and sitting in the backyard enjoying chips and salsa with a side of the great outdoors. Simple togetherness is more important than big doings.

The second language of love that is important to most people is giving the gift of understanding. For most of our lives, many of us have been given confusing messages about our feelings. We have been told to be happy when we aren't. We have been told to stop being mad when we are. So many of us are confused about our feelings and don't know what to do when strong feelings are stirred in our souls.

When someone takes a genuine interest in how we feel and—rather than arguing with our feelings—tries to understand how we feel, it can affect us like warm sunshine on a chilly patch of the garden! For most of us it is a rare experience—and it is priceless!

In this chapter we have talked about becoming mature enough to do some perspective taking. Offering someone the gift of understanding is a good way to do this.

For example, picture a wife who has been hurt by an unkind comment from a colleague. An unthinking (and unfeeling) husband might say: "You just need to toughen up. Don't take it personally. In fact, tell that person to jump in the lake."

Our usual response to people feels a little like standing toe-to-toe giving a lecture. We tell people what's wrong with their thinking and what to do with their feelings. This feels like an irritated parent lecturing a three-year-old. Most of us don't like it. We feel further insulted and very lonely.

Showing understanding feels very different. Instead of standing toe-to-toe, understanding puts us side-by-side. We look at the world together. Though I can never fully understand exactly what you feel, I try. That is the essence of compassion.

Showing understanding is so important that the next chapter is dedicated to that subject.

Exercise

Take a few minutes to complete this exercise:

+ Make a list of things you enjoy doing. Share this list with your partner. Look for things you might do together. If your partner is not reading *The Marriage Garden* with you, think about things she or he enjoys doing that the two of you might do together. Also, as you think about things you enjoy doing, what things could you invite your partner to do with you?
+ When has your spouse shown compassion for one of your struggles? Have you shared with your spouse how much that meant to you?
+ What are some of the struggles your spouse has? How can you show understanding with greater compassion?

Gardens and Relationships Both Need Care

Many gardens fail to flourish because of a lack of sunshine. Many plants wilt and wither when they are in the shade. They may also be destroyed if they are planted right in the path of a thoroughfare—we have all seen paths worn in the grass.

Marriages are similar to plants. They need lots of light. They wither and die in the absence of light. But this light is not ordinary daylight. It is the light of positivity.

Research on strong relationships show that healthy relationships typically have five positives for each negative. That means that a partner will express love, appreciation, and affection an average of five times for each correction or complaint that he or she offers.

This is a giant discovery. After decades of looking for the magic bullet in healthy relationships and considering communication, problem solving, similarity, and so on, the magic bullet was found: positivity. When we look for the good and dwell on it, the relationship gets even better.

In fact, partners in strong relationships wear rose-colored glasses. When they have tough times, they tend to say: "This is temporary. It will pass." When good things happen, positive partners say, "This is it! This is why I am lucky to be married to my partner!" This is not objective analysis. This is the choice to look for the good and celebrate it. In fact some scholars believe the best advice they can give couples is "Hold on to your illusions!" Keep seeing your partner in the favorable light in which you first saw him or her.

The good news is that everyone can find ways to be more positive. Instead of talking about the things that bother us, we can talk about the things we enjoy.

Analyzing the Relationship

There are three parts to every relationship:

+   There are the things I like about my partner that don't need to change.

74

- There are the things I don't like about my partner that never will change.
- There are the things I don't like about my partner that can change.

Our estimate is that most of us like about 80 percent of our partners' personalities. Maybe you love your wife's enthusiasm— even if she is forgetful. Maybe you appreciate your husband's sense of style even if he isn't very good with money. That would leave 20 percent that each of us wishes were different about our partners.

What happens if we think and talk a lot about the things we *do* like about our partners? As we think and talk about the good, we appreciate our partners even more. We feel more loving. Our relationship grows.

What happens if we think and talk a lot about the things we don't like about our partners? If we think and talk a lot about the things we don't like, they fill our minds until it seems like there is nothing good about our partners. Our relationships become dark and hopeless when we allow thoughts about our spouses' faults to overshadow and eclipse all the good that is in them. This may even be true if we spend a lot of time confessing our partners' faults to friends and counselors.

If you're like most of us, you can readily think of times when you have dwelt on the irritants in your relationship. It is a wonderfully effective way to destroy a relationship. Often we think about the irritants in the misguided hope that we can eradicate them. This turns out to be a fool's errand.

John Gottman found that approximately 70 percent of what we don't like about our partners will never change. These may be such things as different personalities, food preferences, or our individual styles. Some things simply won't change! We can talk about them, complain about them, nag about them, and even threaten about them, but these things aren't going to change. Most of what I don't like about my partner (or any partner I may ever have) simply will not change. That is the reality of marriage between humans.

If you are good at math, you recognize that 30 percent of what you don't like *can* change. This sparks hope! Maybe I can fix at least some of my partner's bothersome quirks!

Yet there is a conspiracy of nature that thwarts our hopes. Research shows that the only way to get our partners to change is by loving them the way they are. When we enjoy their goodness, they get even better! When we carp about their faults, they never change. In fact they can take over our minds and hearts so that we lose track of all the things that originally attracted us to the people we married.

Talking about our discontents doesn't cause our partners to improve. But enjoying, appreciating, and loving our partners refocuses our attention. It fills us with appreciation and helps our partners grow in ways that cause us to love them more!

Instead of complaining about a messy kitchen, I might appreciate a lovely meal. Instead of complaining about socks left on the floor, I might pick them up and be grateful for the feet that wear them.

What can we do to keep our minds fixed on the positive? We can keep handy (maybe in our wallets) a list of qualities we enjoy in our partners. We can also make a list of the great experiences we have shared. When we are feeling irritated or frustrated, we might pull out the lists and think about good qualities and good times. We might also put pictures, notes, gifts, or other reminders on our desks or in our workplaces to help us remember the good we see in our spouses.

The way we think about our partners has a very big impact on how we feel about them. We can choose to dwell on the good. Then it will be quite natural to be positive and loving in the things we say.

Reflection

Take a few minutes to respond to these questions:

- What are some of the things you enjoy about your spouse? What can you do to help you be mindful and appreciative of these things? Some possibilities include:
  - Show interest.
  - Be affectionate.
  - Show you care.
  - Be appreciative.
  - Show your concern.
  - Be empathic.
  - Be accepting.
  - Joke around.
  - Share your joy.
- What are the best ways for you to increase the positivity in your relationship?

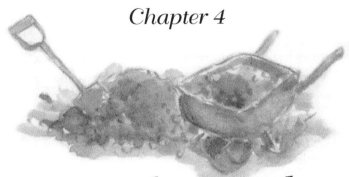

Chapter 4

Understand

Cultivate Compassion for Your Partner

Compassionate understanding of each other is a key to a healthy marriage.
—ANDY CHRISTENSEN AND NEIL JACOBSON

When you let your mate know that you understand his or her feelings and consider them valid, it's as if you opened the door to welcome your partner.
—JOHN GOTTMAN

You don't marry one person; you marry three: the person you think they are, the person they are, and the person they are going to become as a result of being married to you.
—RICHARD NEEDHAM

G ardening can be both rewarding and challenging. At times each of us will get sunburned, poked by thorns, and bitten by bugs. During these difficult and painful times, we can be gardening partners who compassionately respond to each other's pains rather than scold one another for not using sunscreen or being more careful. We can be gardeners in whose gentle hands our partners heal and grow strong. This chapter will focus on four keys to cultivating compassion and understanding for your partner:

1. Getting to know your spouse—and continuing to learn about him or her
2. Listening and responding effectively to your spouse
3. Seeing the world through your spouse's eyes
4. Expressing acceptance and forgiveness

Getting to Know Your Spouse

One of the greatest difficulties in building relationships is that we cannot always see clearly or completely within the heart, mind, and experience of another person. This is especially problematic in marriage where, based on years (or sometimes just months) of experience, we think we know our partners completely. However, understanding our spouses does not happen overnight, just like great gardeners don't learn everything about growing a successful garden in one season. Skilled gardeners take note of those things that work well and repeat them. They also are willing to try new things and seek advice from trusted gardening experts when a part of their garden seems to be struggling. As they do this over time, they gain understanding of how to grow the best gardens they can.

Relationship expert Scott Stanley talks about the difference between "knowing" our spouses and "no-ing" our spouses. He points out that many couples spend too much time telling each other "No." For example, you may frequently hear, or find yourself saying things like "No, I don't want to do that," "No, you don't know what you're talking about," "No, you don't know how I feel," and so forth. All that "no-ing" does little to help you better under-stand your partner and build your marriage garden. In contrast, when we focus on "knowing" or understanding our partners, our gardens begin to flourish.

For example, if a guy from the city marries a girl from the country they can use their different family backgrounds as an excuse to "no" one another or as an opportunity to "know" one another. Their different uses of language or ways of doing things could cause them to be annoyed by one another. These differ-ences could lead to a lot of "no-ing." Or they can get to know each other's families, their history, their pets, and come to appreciate the unique meaning and culture that helped make each of them who they are.

Reflection

Think of times when you are inclined to "no" your spouse—to dismiss or disagree with him or her. In what ways can you turn that "no-ing" into knowing? How can you learn to better understand and appreciate the unique person who is your partner?

Whether you have been married for four months or forty years, there are a variety of ways to get to know your partner better. Try the methods that sound interesting and that you think will work for you. As you and your partner seek to better under-stand one another, your relationship will flourish.

Practice Relationship-Building Talk

Plan a time each day when you and your partner will participate in relationship-building talk for ten to fifteen minutes. Relationship-building talk is different from business talk. Business talk is where things like budgets, bills, appointments, and schedules get discussed. Business talk is important and it is necessary for a household to run smoothly. But business talk doesn't typically build relationships in the same way as relationship-building talk.

Relationship-building talk is the type of talk you probably participated in when you were dating and engaged. It's the type of talk that helped you get to the point that you knew you wanted to get married in the first place. Remember when you were so interested in your partner that you spent hours talking and getting to know each other? Relationship-building talk is about connecting with your partner. It is your opportunity to discuss your hopes and dreams or whatever you would like on a daily basis. Relationship-building talk helps you connect in a different and more profound way than business talk. Although it's not likely, or realistic, that you will spend as much time doing relationship-building talk as you did when you were dating, it is realistic to spend ten to fifteen minutes a day doing it. Relationship-building talk is similar to the daily care and nurturing that gardens need to remain healthy.

One of the best ways to do relationship-building talk is within the context of some other activity. For example, in my (James) work as a marriage therapist, I once had a female client tell me, "My husband just doesn't talk to me. It is so frustrating."

I asked her to think of an exception, of a time when he did seem to open up and talk more than usual. After considerable thought she said, "He does seem to talk more whenever we go on a road trip together." I asked her why she thought her husband talked more than usual on those trips. She said, "I think it's because he's focused on driving and he's looking at the road rather than looking straight at me. I think he's more comfortable that way."

I invited this woman and her husband to take a nightly drive (this was when gas cost less than $1.50 a gallon) and to use that time as their opportunity to do relationship-building talk. It worked. She later reported that those nightly drives had helped her and her husband get to know one another better.

Another couple I worked with used a morning cup of coffee as their time to do relationship-building talk. A couple I know sits in their hot tub for a few minutes almost every night as their time for relationship-building talk. Some couples take a daily walk together. My wife and I have a nightly bedtime snack, after the kids are in bed, and use that as our opportunity to talk. Wally and Nancy use drive time to and from work to reconnect. They talk about what they did during the day and also how they're feeling about life and work.

Identify the time, place, or activity that will work for you to do relationship-building talk. If you don't schedule the time and the place, it will not happen. If you do relationship-building talk consistently, you will find that your relationship will grow because you are putting energy into connecting with and learning about your partner. John Gottman put it this way, "Working briefly on your marriage every day will do more for your health and longevity than working out at a health club."

For some people, relationship-building talk will come easily. They just need to make the time to do it each day. Other people may be thinking, "I'm willing to try relationship-building talk, but what in the world will we talk about?" If this sounds like you, here are some ideas to get you started with relationship-building talk.

- **Ask Me a Question.** Although you may feel like you know your partner very well, you'd be surprised how much more there is to learn. You and your partner can each think of one new question every day that you would like to know the answer to. When you and your partner talk, take turns asking each other the questions you have thought of. This should start some great, and occasionally even difficult, conversations. Be creative in developing meaningful questions and remember that you may not even know the answers about some of your partner's basic preferences (for example, favorite color, food, pet, time of year, music, movie, date, and so on). Here are some questions you can use to get you started.

  1. Who are your best friends (past and present)?
  2. What was your most stressful childhood event?
  3. What was your most embarrassing moment?
  4. What would you do if you suddenly inherited a lot of money or won the lottery?
  5. What would be your ideal job?
  6. What would be your ideal place to live?
  7. What are some things that currently cause you stress?
  8. What are some of your life dreams?
  9. Who are your favorite and least favorite relatives?
  10. What strengthens trust with you?
  11. What undermines trust with you?

- **Confused in Colorado (Dear Abby Game).** Family life professor Stephen Duncan recommends choosing an advice column from your local newspaper, such as Ann Landers or Dear Abby, and reading the question—but not the answer—aloud to one another. Once you have read the question, take turns giving advice and your reasons for the advice. Do this without criticizing, insulting, or making fun of one another—that is, "no-ing" each other. This is a great way to communicate, get to know each other better, and understand how your partner may respond in different situations.

Build Traditions of Connection

Traditions are things that we get in the habit of doing. They usually have some special meaning and significance for us. In marriage we should get in the habit of connecting with our partners frequently and in a variety of ways (spiritually, emotionally, and physically). Experienced gardeners have certain traditions they follow every year. These are things they are in the habit of doing because they help ensure a bountiful harvest. They might include such things as tilling the garden and adding soil conditioners each year, starting seeds indoors during cold weather so seedlings are ready to be planted outside when the threat of frost has passed, planting tomatoes deep, planting spinach and peas early, and so forth. Here are just a few ideas of marital traditions that you and your partner may want to start in order to stay connected and better understand one another.

- **Find the Glory in Your Marital Story.** One of the most important and powerful traditions for couples to adopt are the practice of finding and recounting the glory of their marital story. John Gottman encourages couples to recall the positive history of their relationship as a way to bond with one another.

  As a therapist, I have met with many couples who seem to have forgotten the reasons they got married in the first place or why they even liked each other. Often these couples come in for counseling with their hearts aching and hardened toward one another. Usually these couples have spent significant time rewriting their relationship histories in negative ways and almost no time nurturing the good to be found in their relationships. In this difficult state, they are then tempted to begin sharing with me the negative history they have been cultivating. Rather than allowing them to rehearse this negative history endlessly, I invite them to consider a different, more positive story.

One of the most powerful interventions I use to get these couples thinking positively is to have them tell me the story of how they met, fell in love, and decided to get married. Often by the time they are done sharing these accounts, their hearts have changed, they have softened, and they have a renewed desire to preserve and strengthen their relationship. On more than one occasion I have observed couples reaching out for one another's hands as they recall and recount the glory of their marital story. As the frozen hardness of their hearts begins to crack and melt toward one another, I see them seeking to reconnect physically as their hearts are reconnecting emotionally. Finding and sharing the glory of your marital story truly is the Miracle-Gro of vibrant marriage gardens.

Even if you are not having trouble in your marriage, sharing stories of your love and courtship with one another and with others will help you stay connected and committed. A great way to share the glory of your marital story is through physical and verbal reminders of your commitments to one another. For example, you can take time to occasionally look through wedding photos together, you can share stories of the fun times you've had or the trials you have overcome, or you can talk about keepsakes that have a special meaning in your relationship. Rebecca Simon shared the following example.

The Red-Handled School Bell

Prominently placed on a shelf in my parent's home sits a red-handled school bell. As a child, I was curious about the bell, and I asked my mother why we had it or what was so special about it. She just smiled and said, "It's a good reminder." She then explained that the bell had been given to her and my dad on their wedding day by my uncle Raymond, who was the priest who married them. She said the bell had a special meaning for them, but when I was a child, she did not tell me what it was.

As a young girl, I hoped that my uncle Raymond would be able to officiate at my wedding ceremony some day, just like he had for my parents. Unfortunately, he passed away before I met my husband. However, on the day of my wedding, right after my husband, Kenny, and I had exchanged our vows, our priest, Father William, said he had something for us. In front of our family and friends, Father William handed us a red-handled school bell. He then explained to us that my parents had requested that we be given the bell as a reminder of Father Raymond and the advice he would always give newly married couples, "Be good to one another, and if there is ever an argument, ring that bell. Ringing the bell will make you stop and really think about why you are fighting."

Receiving the bell, and learning of its significance, on my wedding day was one of the most touching gifts I had ever received from my parents. The bell hasn't been used very much, but I can say that when it does, I am immediately reminded of Father Raymond's words, "Be good to one another." Those comforting words help us calm down and work through our differences.

Share the glory of your marital story with your children, friends, dinner guests, or anyone who is willing to listen. The more you share it, the stronger your feelings for one another will grow.

Make Time to Share Special Connections

- **Share Intimacy.** Plan romantic and intimate times with your partner. Spontaneity is great, but planning a date or other romantic event with your partner can be just as much fun as the date itself, and it creates something to look forward to.
- **Share Spirituality.** Shared religious or spiritual activities are a wonderful way to grow together as a couple. The way you express your spirituality is up to you, but you may want to consider praying, reading inspiring religious books, attending church services, and celebrating religious holidays together.

- **Happy Anniversary!** Anniversaries are a big deal. Remember them and make them special. In addition to the day you got married, you can also celebrate the anniversary of your first date, the first time you kissed your partner, or the time you knew you were in love. Be creative with the anniversaries you celebrate and the ways you celebrate them.

- **"I Love You" Codes.** Develop subtle or indirect ways of letting your partner know you love them. For example, a couple I know will squeeze each other's hand three times representing the words "I-Love-You." In response to those three squeezes, the other person will squeeze four times, representing the words "I-Love-You-More." The final response is five squeezes. That means "I-Love-You-the-Most." This is a sweet and simple way that this couple has identified to express their affection for each other. It helps them to build their emotional intimacy. They have also sent the same messages to each other by winking, honking the car horn, or turning the porch light on and off. What's your "I love you" code?

- **Frequently Connect with Your Partner.**
  Use brief phone calls or e-mails to connect with your partner throughout the day. Let them know you care about them or were just thinking about them.

- **Do Your Partner's Favorite Thing.** Let your partner know you care by doing one of his or her favorite things. It doesn't have to be big. For example, bring home a card, a favorite treat, or write a simple note.

- **Think "Partner First."** Although self-care is important, partner care is equally important. Think about and do the things that will show your partner that he or she is your number one priority. Losing yourself in serving your partner will help you better understand both your partner and yourself.

- **Five-Minute Connections.** With the business of life, couples often have little time to spend with one another. When quantity time is not available, John Gottman recommends making five-minute connections with your partner as often as you can. Here's how:

  - **Cuddle at the most important time of day.** Set the alarm five minutes early and cuddle with your partner in the morning. It can help keep you feeling close all day long.

  - **Before you leave in the morning, ask your partner if anything special is going on that day.** This lets your partner know that you are interested in her and care what's going on in her life. If something special was going on for your partner, check in with her during the day or in the evening.

  - **Share what you like about each other.** Do this daily and do it frequently. Let your partner know all the things you love and admire about him. Your partner will know he is loved and will be more willing to work through any differences you may have.

  - **Do small acts of kindness for one another.** Send your partner a card or e-mail just to say you love her, bring home a special treat, or do a five-minute chore that your partner usually does. The kindness you show to your partner will almost always be returned, and serving your partner will strengthen your marriage bond.

- **Talk about the stresses of your day.** Spend five minutes when you get home from work talking with your partner about the stressful things you may have experienced that day. Don't attack your partner with it; just share it with him. If you get the stress out of the way first, you will be able to enjoy the rest of the evening together.

Listening and Responding Effectively to Your Spouse

Maybe you're the kind of gardener that we are. The bugs and weather would have to destroy a plant down to the ground before we would notice something was wrong. We entirely miss the subtle cues like wilting and chewed leaves along the way. Sometimes we're the same way in our marriages. Our partners are giving many clues about their needs, but we don't notice until the relationship is almost dead.

When our partners talk to us, it is important to listen carefully to what they have to say. Even when we have known our spouses for many years, we usually are only partly right about what they are thinking or experiencing. When our partners speak to us they are hopeful that we will be attentive to them and care enough to understand them. They are hopeful that we will respond in a way that opens up a conversation. This section will focus on three important aspects of careful listening: listening carefully during calm times, listening carefully to strong emotions, and listening carefully to hopes for the future.

Listening Carefully During Calm Times

When our spouses speak calmly to us, it may seem easy to respond in appropriate and effective ways, but sometimes we still miss the opportunity. As John Gottman puts it, we must be willing to pay attention to our partners' "bids" for connection. A bid is any effort our partners make to communicate with us or strike up a conversation.

One time my wife, Kathie, and I were on a long road trip. Kathie had been reading a book in the passenger seat while I was driving. Out of the blue she asked me if I was thirsty. I wasn't, so I simply responded, "No." Although I had heard the question that Kathie had asked and had responded, I didn't really understand what she was asking. I was not listening carefully. I had made no effort to understand Kathie's bid for connection or to continue the conversation.

A few moments after my response, I realized that rather than reading her book Kathie was now staring at me. She had a look of amused disbelief on her face. Initially, I gave her one of those looks that says, "What's up?" and then I figured it out, better late than never. Although I wasn't thirsty and my response had been genuine, I had not bothered to figure out what the question meant to my wife. I finally realized that Kathie was thirsty and that it might be a good time to stop for a rest and a drink.

Listening Carefully and Responding to a Partner's Strong Emotions

When our spouses sound frustrated or angry (whether we think it's with us or with someone else) it can be more difficult to listen carefully and try to understand what they are feeling. But even then, it's important to be willing to listen past the edge in our partners' voices. A good listener is one who seeks to understand what his partner is thinking and feeling, rather than assuming he already knows. Here's an example of how making assumptions can cause problems.

In the midst of her evening routine a wife might exclaim to her husband in a frustrated tone, "I am so tired." The husband may think he knows why she is tired. He may believe that her tiredness comes from staying up too late or from new demands at her job. If he offers her unsolicited advice—such as "Why don't you go to bed earlier?" or "Why don't you delegate some of your old duties at work?"—he will almost certainly miss the mark. Although his counsel may be well intended, it may not be welcome.

So, what might this husband do differently? When his partner expresses tiredness, pain, or any other strong emotion, this husband could offer support rather than advice. He could avoid the temptation to impose his own meanings on his wife's words and experiences. He could avoid trying to solve her problems, unless she has specifically asked for suggestions. Instead, he could simply respond to the message she has given him in a way that is not presumptuous and invites more discussion. For example, he might say: "Sounds like you feel overwhelmed. Is there anything I can do to help?" or "Tell me more, dear," or "Sounds like you've had a tough day."

Any effort on this husband's part to open the door for his wife to tell him more will probably be helpful. She might say, "Everything went wrong at work today," or "I'm worn out when I get home from work," or "I guess I feel pretty lonely." Even with this additional information, a husband is wise to keep listening. Nodding and listening may encourage her to keep sharing. Keep the focus on what she is feeling rather than giving advice or telling her about your experience.

As the conversation continues, this husband might do the following things to continue listening to and supporting his spouse.

- **Validate her emotions.** Some validating responses might include, "I can see why you would feel that way," or "No wonder you feel bad," or "I don't know how you have tolerated it this long." When a partner feels strong emotions, it is a good time to listen and support. As the emotions lessen, it may be helpful to ask your partner how you can help: "Do you want me to just listen or would you like me to help you brainstorm solutions?"

  It is important to keep in mind that people find it almost impossible to respond with validation when they feel attacked. We will all react and bite back at times. We will talk more about how to handle tense situations in the next chapter on problem solving—but if we learn to listen for the bid for connection, we can avoid a lot of fights.

- **Express affection.** Tell your partner "I'm sorry you're going through this. I love you." Understanding and the support it conveys are very healing. In fact, there is hardly anything a marriage partner can do regularly that will build a relationship as much as being understanding.

- **Respond to the need.** If your spouse says that she needs someone to help prepare dinner, move from words to actions. Grab the potato peeler and start peeling.

Because the pain and frustration of others often makes us uncomfortable, it is natural that we respond to it with advice, distractions, or other efforts to minimize the pain. Unfortunately, this is probably not what our partners need or want from us. Although it may not be natural or easy for us to respond to pain with understanding and compassion, it can be learned. And it can make a big difference for each partner and for the relationship.

Reflection

Do you notice and try to understand when your partner has strong feelings? Think about the times that your partner has shared pain, disappointment, or frustration with you. What are your usual responses? Many of us automatically say unhelpful things. Notice if you find yourself using any of the following *unhelpful* responses:

+ Giving advice: "What you need to do is . . ."
+ Talking about your own feelings and experiences instead of theirs: "That same thing happened to me. . . ."
+ Making their pain seem unimportant: "Everyone suffers. What makes you so special?"

Maybe you sometimes have used good listening skills. See if you have used (or are ready to try) some of the following *helpful* ways of showing understanding:

+ Acknowledge your partner's feelings: "I can see that you feel strongly about this."
+ Invite more discussion: "I would like to understand. Please tell me more."
+ Acknowledge that your partner's pain is real for him or her: "You must feel awful."

Listening in order to understand is difficult. It takes time and patience. It requires us to get outside our own thoughts, preferences, and point of view. This takes deliberate effort. During the coming weeks, try to notice when your partner has strong feelings about something. Instead of giving advice or talking about your experiences, try using the helpful ways to show understanding listed above. Practice preliving the experience so it comes more naturally when an opportunity presents itself. By truly listening to our partners and responding effectively to what they tell us, we encourage our marriages to grow.

Listening Carefully and Responding to a Partner's Hopes for the Future

Acknowledging and respecting each other's deepest, most personal hopes and dreams is the key to saving and enriching your marriage.
—JOHN GOTTMAN

In happy marriages partners incorporate each other's goals into their concept of what their marriage is about.
—JOHN GOTTMAN

Part of understanding our spouses is to honor their hopes and dreams, even if we don't always share them or they don't seem realistic to us. For example, if finances are tight and your spouse says, "It sure would be fun to go to Hawaii," you may respond in a variety of ways. One way is to angrily or disbelievingly say, "With what money?" This type of response does not honor your spouse's dream. Your spouse is probably keenly aware that finances would not allow you to travel to Hawaii, but he or she was inviting you to dream together anyway.

Some responses that would honor your spouse's statement about going to Hawaii might be, "That sure would be fun. Let's try and figure out a way that we can go someday" or "That will be fun when we can go. For now shall we look at pictures of Hawaii on the Web or go out for a Hawaiian dinner?"

Here is another example. I have always wanted a truck, but timing and circumstances have made it impractical for me to own one. One of the things I appreciate about my wife, Kathie, is her willingness to honor my desire to have a truck someday. Whenever I see a nice truck and say something about how pretty it is, she says, "I wish I could buy you a truck," and I know she means it. Her willingness to honor in fantasy a dream that she can't grant me in reality is more important and more valuable than the truck itself.

We honor our spouses' hopes and dreams by being willing to listen to those dreams, understand them, and incorporate our spouses' preferences into our actions. Understanding partners work to incorporate each other's dreams into their marriage relationship. They are also willing and flexible enough to change as they grow and develop individually and as a couple.

Some couples have a stable marriage even when their hopes and dreams aren't completely in sync (for example, they have different levels of religiosity, they have different preferences for where they would like to live, and so on). However, the more shared hopes and dreams you have and the more you seek to understand one another, the more meaningful, rich, and fulfilling your relationship will be.

Reflection

Take a few minutes to respond to this question:

+ What is one of your spouse's hopes or dreams that you can
honor simply by being willing to talk to him or her about it?

Seeing the World Through Your Partner's Eyes

*Encouraging your partner to speak is an act of generosity. It is a gift
of your attention and interest. You are granting that your spouse has
something worthwhile to say. Granting the legitimacy of your partner's
point of view is a precious gift at any time.*

—JOHN GOTTMAN

Most of us are keenly aware of our own wants, needs, hopes,
dreams, fears, and desires. However, we usually are much less
attuned to our partners' wants, needs, hopes, dreams, fears, and
desires. We find it difficult to truly "walk a mile in their shoes." To
do this takes skill, but more important, it takes willingness. It is
much like Steve Covey's recommendation to "seek first to understand . . . then to be understood."

In the *Seven Habits of Highly Effective People*, Covey tells the story
of what he thought was his wife's unreasonable love for Frigidaire
appliances. He could never understand it. Nor could he dissuade
her. It was not until he was willing to let her explore her feelings
about Frigidaire that they discovered the reason for her loyalty.

98

When she was a young girl, Sandra's father operated an appliance store. During a time of economic difficulty, the Frigidaire company was willing to finance her father's inventory. That allowed him to stay in business. It made a big difference for her family. Once Covey made time for his wife to speak openly about her feelings and himself to understand his wife's family history with Frigidaire appliances, he was able to see more clearly through her eyes.

Consider how you would respond to the following story that has been adapted from Dr. Haim Ginott's *Between Parent and Child*.

Understanding Burnt Toast

Scenario 1

It's a busy morning as a young couple with a new baby struggles to get ready for the day. It is one of those mornings when everything seems to go wrong. The telephone rings, the baby cries, and the toast that the wife was preparing for breakfast gets burnt. Imagine that her husband rushes over to the toaster and says: "Good grief! When will you ever learn to make toast?"

Put yourself in the place of the wife who has been criticized for burning the toast.

* How might you react? (Would you throw the toast at your spouse? Would you shout, "Well then, fix your own toast"? Would you be so upset you'd feel like crying or shouting a rude comment in return?)
* What would your spouse's words make you feel toward him or her? (Anger, hate, resentment?)

- Would it be emotionally easy for you to fix another batch of toast at that moment?
- And when you went your way for the day, would it be easy to concentrate on other tasks? (Would the whole day be ruined?)

Scenario 2

Now let's replay the scene again. Suppose that the situation is the same—the toast is burnt, but this time, the husband, upon seeing the burnt toast, gets the loaf of bread and says calmly to his wife, "Let me show you, honey, how to make toast."

Put yourself in the place of the wife once again. How might you react to scenario 2? Would you feel worse than the first scenario because now it seems that your spouse is treating you like you are stupid?

Scenario 3

Let's replay the busy morning scene one last time. Everything is still the same, but this time the husband says, "Gee, honey, it's been a rough morning for you—the baby, the phone, and now the toast. Would you like me to make some more toast?"

Put yourself in the place of the wife one last time.

How might you react to scenario 3? Would you drop dead from shock? Would you feel wonderful and loved? Would you feel so good that you'd want to hug and kiss your spouse?

Think about your reaction to each scenario. Was your reaction different in the third scenario than in the first two? If so, why? What would make the difference? The morning was still crazy. The baby was still crying and the toast was still burnt.

In the third scenario you may be thinking that all those other things wouldn't matter that much. You might feel grateful that your spouse didn't criticize you—that he or she was with you, not against you. And you'd probably find it much easier to concentrate on other tasks throughout the rest of the day.

Walking in the shoes of your partner—even for a few moments—means admitting that your partner's view might be reasonable and understandable. Allowing ourselves to see from our partners' perspective dispels past misunderstandings, enabling trust and compassion to flourish. Giving the gift of understanding to our spouses is as refreshing and vital as cool water is to a parched plant.

Honey, I'm Home

Julia had gotten home from work late and looked at the clock. Ouch. Her husband would be there any minute. He was a long-distance truck driver who was gone three to four days at a time. He was due back from his latest trip at 6:00 PM or so, and her tradition was to celebrate the beginning of several days together with a special dinner. She loved doing it. She would even light candles and use their only linen tablecloth.

But now she had only fifteen minutes to start a meal and get everything else ready. At 6:15 she actually was relieved he still had not arrived. It gave her the chance to get the food going. Nevertheless, all too soon she heard the air brakes bleat as he brought the eighteen-wheeler to a stop in front of the house. She began biting her lip. She could imagine him taking off his boots in the utility room, hanging up his coat, and calling out to her. She knew his face would fall when he saw the half-set table and no food.

The door opened, the boots were unlaced, and the coat was hung up. He called out: "Hey, Jenny." She automatically yelled back, "Hi, Hon." She inhaled in anticipation of his disappointed look as he glanced around the corner into the kitchen. He looked at the table. He gazed up at her, broke into a big smile and bellowed, "Well, it looks like I got home just in time to help!" All her fears dissolved.

Reflection

Think about a time when someone was willing to "see things through your eyes." What effect did this have on your relationship with that person?

Expressing Acceptance and Forgiveness

A happy marriage is the union of two good forgivers.
—Robert Quillen

Forgiveness is the fragrance the violet sends out to the heel that crushed it.
—Mark Twain

As humans, we all make mistakes. Sometimes we forget to water our gardens for a few days. Sometimes we spill too much fertilizer on a plant and burn it. Sometimes we think we are reaching for a weed, but we pull up a plant by mistake. When this happens, we may wish we could turn back the clock. We may wish for a "do over." We may also hope for acceptance and forgiveness from those whom we have offended or injured.

Little Things

Both acceptance and forgiveness are essential parts of any significant long-term relationship. Relationship expert Blaine Fowers points out that if spouses cannot accept and forgive one another for weaknesses and mistakes, then hurt and disappointment will build and damage the relationship. In his book, *Beyond the Myth of Marital Happiness*, Fowers shares a touching account of acceptance and forgiveness in the daily life of a couple.

> One day a woman was visiting a friend of hers who had recently celebrated her fifty-fourth wedding anniversary. During their conversation the woman's husband came into the house wearing his work boots. He left clods of dirt behind him on the spotless kitchen floor. The visitor expected that the wife would be upset as she commented, "His boots certainly do bring the dirt in." As the wife got up to get the broom, she said with a smile, "Yes, but they bring him in too."

What was it about this woman who had been married fifty-four years that allowed her to respond the way she did? Was she a saint? Was she a slave to her husband? Was she crazy? I doubt any of these is true. It is more likely that after fifty-four years of marriage she has learned not to take offense at small annoyances. She has learned that her relationship with her husband is more important than a little dirt.

Some may ask, "Do the wife's actions absolve her husband of his responsibility to be more neat—to not track dirt into the house?" The answer is no. Undoubtedly, the husband could have been more careful. He probably should have removed his boots before entering the house. However, this story teaches us that in marriage, mercy, compassion, and a willingness not to take offense are more potent nutrients of a healthy marriage than the poisons of bitterness and taking offense.

Bigger Things

Sometimes our mistakes are more serious and costly than a little mud on the kitchen floor. At these times we may wonder, can I still accept what has happened? Can I forgive?

The answer is yes. You may be thinking of some personal examples of acceptance and forgiveness right now. Let me share an example from my life. Five years ago my family lived in a very cold and snowy part of the country. One particularly snowy morning I was involved in a car wreck. It was nothing too serious. No one was injured. But the front grill of my car was smashed, a headlight was broken, and the hood resembled a taco shell.

Because the car was still drivable, after pushing the hood back down, I continued on to work. Upon arriving at work, I got sucked into some meetings and other responsibilities I had that morning. Not more than a couple hours after my crash, my

overzealous insurance agent called my home to get some details
of the damages. My wife answered. Unfortunately, with the
businesses of the morning I had not yet called her to tell her what
happened. Needless to say, the news of my accident came as a
shock to her. At that point, she could have had several reasons to
be upset with me. First, I had wrecked the car. Second, I hadn't
called to tell her about it. Third, she found out about the accident
from our insurance agent.

One of the amazing and wonderful things about my wife,
though, is that she did not get mad. She called me right after
she got off the phone with our insurance agent. She didn't say,
"You idiot! Why did you wreck the car?" She didn't say, "You
idiot! Why didn't you call me to tell me you were in an accident?"
Instead, her first words were simple. They were caring. They let
me know that I mattered to her more than anything else. Her
first words were, "Are *you* OK?" I love her for her acceptance
of both what I had and hadn't done. I love her willingness to
forgive.

Another example of the healing power of compassion and
a willingness to accept and forgive one's spouse is illustrated in
the following story that was shared by one of our team members,
Katie Baney. She said,

> We all do dumb things, and I am no exception. I have a car
> with a handy-dandy backup camera, but that really does
> you no good if you don't look in the monitor. While backing
> out of my garage the other day, I was more concerned with
> avoiding a turtle, and watching him, than with my backup
> camera. I suddenly felt a jar and heard a crash, and realized
> I had just backed into a fence. This just added to an already
> bad day. I decided the best thing for me to do was to go by

and see my wonderful husband, John, and ask for a hug. When I got there and saw him I already felt better, but I was still anxious about what his reaction to me wrecking the car would be. I told him what happened and showed him the damage and he said "Well, is the turtle OK?" I smiled, and knew that not only was the turtle OK, but so was I.

Learning Acceptance and Forgiveness

If you think it may be difficult for you to learn to be more accepting and forgiving of your partner, maybe the following strategy shared by relationship expert, Sam Bradley, will help. During a marriage workshop, he described how he cured himself of his habit of taking offense at his wife. He described himself as being very neat and his wife as being very messy. He said he cured himself from his annoyance with her messiness by imagining that she had died and then asking himself, "If I could bring her back but she'd still be messy, leave clutter all over the house—five pairs of shoes in the living room—would I still want her back?" He said he would absolutely want her back because the messes didn't matter nearly as much as having her in his life. That cured him. Whenever he gets annoyed with her mess, he just asks himself that question again.

Accepting our spouses for who they are and being willing to overlook little things that annoy us is a precious gift. Our willingness to accept our spouses, warts and all, nurtures the relationship and enables growth and change we previously thought impossible. A woman I know told me the following story.

I Was Different

One day I left the dinner table distraught over my husband's inability to understand my feelings. I was so tired of his insensitivity. I couldn't tell whether he was just dense or deliberately ignoring me. On top of that, he was so verbally inarticulate I began to doubt at times how or why we ever got married. "If we had communicated this poorly before we were married," I thought, "how did we ever manage to utter and accept a proposal!" I stalked upstairs to sulk in the bedroom.

In a few minutes I heard a soft knock at the door. Of course I didn't answer, and turned my back as he pushed open the half-closed door. I could tell he was standing in the middle of the room. He began stuttering something incoherent: "I uh . . . Maybe we could . . . Would you . . . Could I . . . I mean . . . I wonder . . . Hon, I . . ."

I felt suddenly strange. In an instant I no longer was enjoying his predicament. Earlier, I thought I would relish his pitiful attempt to make up. But now I saw only a man who didn't know how to express his feelings very well struggling to express his feelings. I turned suddenly and interrupted him: I blurted out, "Jake, thank you. I feel bad too. I'm sorry."

I know that if the communication police had been there they would have criticized me for

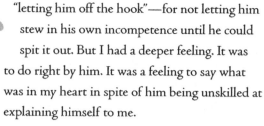

"letting him off the hook"—for not letting him stew in his own incompetence until he could spit it out. But I had a deeper feeling. It was to do right by him. It was a feeling to say what was in my heart in spite of him being unskilled at explaining himself to me.

What is interesting about this event is that from that day forward he began to be more verbal. He was still halting and unsure at times, but he tried harder. And, in a way, I was different. I was less insistent that he "do or say it my way." I was less ready to take offense when he seemed oblivious to my concerns. I must have quit accusing him in my heart. I began looking for how I could make things better. It seems to me that he had so much more to say when I was less demanding that he say it. I probably changed more that day than he did—but we have both changed.

Reflection

Take a few minutes to respond to these questions:

◆ Is there a habit, mannerism, or behavior that your spouse engages in that bothers you? What would it mean to your spouse and to your relationship if you chose to ignore this thing and accept your spouse the way he or she is?

Exercise

During the coming week(s), what will you do to better understand your spouse? List one or two things you would like to do. Make a specific plan and rehearse it in your mind—that is, prelive the experience.

For example, you may decide to give the gift of compassion when your spouse is having a tough day. You may decide to ask your spouse one new question each day to find out more about him or her. Picture specific things you will do. Imagine the likely response. Prepare yourself to handle any difficulties. In your mind, practice several times carrying out your plan.

Chapter 5

Solve

Turn Differences into Blessings

You can't make a marriage work if all you care
about is what makes you happy.
—MICHELE WEINER-DAVIS

Often the difference between a successful marriage
and a mediocre one consists of leaving about
three or four things a day unsaid.
—HARLAN MILLER

We may have very different visions for our shared gardens. One gardener may favor colorful annuals while the other insists on fruit trees. These differences may not simply disappear with a calm discussion. Each partnership will have differences that cannot be resolved. If we choose to stay calm, listen attentively, understand our partners' views, and use creativity, it is possible to turn differences into strengths.

There's No Such Thing as a Weed-Free Garden

Weeds and bugs are a normal and natural part of every garden, but they ought not to be the focus. We manage these annoyances as best we can while choosing to focus our energy and attention on the beauty of the flowers.

In marriage, as in gardening, we are most successful when we choose to focus our time and attention on the beauties and wonders of our spouses and our relationships, rather than on the occasional disagreements and conflicts that creep into our gardens. With proper care our marriages, like our gardens, can flourish in spite of those pesky weeds and bugs.

No couple agrees on everything or gets along with each other 100 percent of the time. In fact, little irritations and periodic battles are normal. If you've been married longer than five minutes, you probably know this. Some conflicts are likely in marriage simply because married couples are so close and they deal with more things together than with anyone else. This closeness and sharing of experiences also makes marriage one of the most rewarding and happy relationships we can have.

In fact, John Gottman has found that "happily married couples aren't smarter, richer, or more psychologically astute than other couples." They are simply willing to keep their negative thoughts and feelings about one another from overwhelming their positive thoughts and feelings. In other words, they don't get so obsessed with the weeds and bugs in their marriage gardens that they forget the flowers.

In addition, these happy couples know which problems can be weeded out of their marriage gardens and which ones cannot. As we mentioned in Chapter Three, Gottman has noted that about 70 percent of what we don't like about our partner will never change. We can pester, threaten, or beg, but some aspects of our partner simply are not going to change. Part of having a happy marriage is learning to accept our spouses. We must accept our spouses' imperfections if we hope for them to accept ours.

Marital problems come in two kinds, those that are *resolvable* and those that are *perpetual*. This chapter will focus on helpful "weeding techniques" for those problems that are resolvable and on acceptance strategies for managing those differences that may be perpetual.

Solving the Right Problem

The first step in developing a healthy approach to marital problem solving is making sure that we are addressing the *right* problem. We may often have the misguided view that our spouse is the source, or the cause, of the majority of our relationship problems. We may think that if we could just get our spouses to change in certain key ways then we could be happy. If this is the approach that we take, we'll never be satisfied. We'll always be on the lookout for the next "spousal improvement" project we think we can't live without.

Jonathan Haidt, well-known psychologist and author of the book *The Happiness Hypothesis*, points out that "by seeing the log in your own eye you can become less biased, less moralistic, and therefore less inclined toward argument and conflict." Haidt also suggests that we have greater capacity to understand others and heal relationships when we make a deliberate effort to identify our own fault in any conflict. He recommends a three-step process for doing this:

1. Think of a recent conflict with someone you care about.
2. Identify one way in which your behavior was not exemplary.
3. Extend an apology for your role in the conflict (however small that role might be).

Haidt cautions that we may tend to resist the urge to find fault with ourselves. We may try to tell ourselves that our words or actions were justified. We may believe that the other person's transgression was greater than our own, so we need not take responsibility for our part in it. None of these rationalizations will help heal our relationships. However, as we honestly engage in these three steps we will find that our anger softens and we will invite a spirit of healing and forgiveness into our relationships.

Relationship expert C. Terry Warner has said, "If we do not suspect ourselves of having been wrong, our search for what is right won't be completely sincere." Searching for what is right takes humility and a realization that our view is not the only (or necessarily the best) view.

The power of a change of heart is not mysterious. Warner points out that "when we abandon our resentments, we no longer live in a resentful world. Others become real to us. We have a sense of how they feel and what will please them. And pleasing them is what we desire to do, because we have put away our resentment."

The following story shared by a friend who is a self-proclaimed "sports nut" illustrates the importance of identifying and solving the right problem in marriage. In this story, we initially see that when my friend's heart is accusing and resentful toward his wife, he not only invites the problems they are experiencing to continue, he also invests in those problems. We then are taught that many relationship problems may have simpler solutions than we would expect. But this only seems to be the case when we are willing to see our role in the problem, see the problem from our spouse's perspective, and validate and take seriously his or her concerns and preferences. This means we have to get our hearts right toward our partners in order to have lasting and meaningful solutions to marital differences and problems.

Sports Nut

I had always been a bit of a sports nut when it came to college and professional football. This was a challenge at home because my wife cannot stand football. When the playoffs rolled around she felt she lost me on Saturdays as well as Sundays. Moreover, when I was immersed in a game in front of the TV, I had to have absolute quiet.

Generally, my Saturday contribution to the household chores involved the great outdoors. Often on Saturdays in the early fall, when I had squandered the morning by sleeping late or talking on the phone, my wife would wait until the game had started and then fire up the lawn mower right outside the family room window where I was. She knew I hated to have her do the lawn or, heaven forbid, have the neighbors see her doing it. I think that is why she would mow the front lawn first. Sometimes I would shut the blinds and turn up the TV. Other times, I would go outside and in a truly Oscar-winning martyr performance, forcibly take the lawn mower from her and resentfully attend to the task. I did this all the while telling myself I had a witch for a wife.

Meanwhile, she would storm inside and begin vacuuming—the family room first, of course—so as to be able to remind me later that she had "already done that room," and she didn't want it messed up again. My presence in the room, of course, was what would mess it up. Last fall, each Saturday unfolded more or less like this. Although the exact events would vary, my childish attitude and complaining were the same. This year I geared up for another long string of miserable Saturdays.

One Friday night in late August, my neighbor good-naturedly said to me, "Well, it's just about time for the football wars to start."

I thought he was talking about the start of the college season and agreed that it would be great to see who was going to prevail in the race for the conference crown.

He smiled and said, "Well, yes, that will be interesting too, but not quite as interesting as the wars at your house as to when the lawn will get mown."

I laughed and waved and walked into the house seething. I had no idea the ongoing battle between my wife and me was public knowledge. I tried to tell myself this whole thing was her fault—was a symptom of her obsession about how the lawn needed to be done before anything else. Then I made the mistake of looking in the mirror. It was as if my own face were calling me out. I avoided looking in my own eyes.

The problem was this. I am a manager in a manufacturing plant. I am good at seeing when employees give themselves excuses for not just doing what needs to be done. There I was, doing the same thing at home and feeling justified about it. I had my story down pat.

It was my wife's Nazi-like insistence on messing up my one hobby, my one way to relax, that was my problem. I had to stand firm or I would be trapped doing chores all day long and have no freedom at all. Wait. I was already trapped. I spent so much time resisting getting the lawn done, that I either did take all day doing it, or I would miss the game trying to make sure she didn't embarrass me in front of the neighbors by trying to do it herself. No wonder the neighbors had us figured out. We were on stage every Saturday.

I put my manager hat on at home and examined my behavior as if I had been a recalcitrant employee. The solution was so obvious it was embarrassing. I simply needed to get up early and do the lawn before the game started. What I had seen as my wife's problem became a recognition of my own foolishness. I changed in an instant.

I got up earlier and did the lawn for three straight Saturdays before she came to me and said, "OK. What are you up to? This isn't you." I had to confess that what wasn't me was the way I had been behaving before. I was unwilling to be at home what I prided myself in being at work. The irritation of how we attacked Saturdays was, in this case, a problem of my own creation.

I wish the solutions to differences were always this easy. And yet, other little problems my wife and I had began to look different. This change seemed to have something to do with my willingness to identify and accept my role in our problems—to get my heart right toward my wife—instead of seeking to blame her for all that I thought was wrong in our relationship. It also had something to do with each of us being interested in how we could make a positive change regarding the differences we had. We work through more things now. We are more patient, more willing to laugh, more willing to examine possibilities. Maybe our situation has changed only slightly. But who we are with each other has changed greatly.

Perspective Taking

Honestly try to put yourself in the place of your spouse. Try to see, feel, and experience whatever issues your spouse may struggle with as he or she does. This can be a difficult thing to do because most of us assume we are seeing the world correctly. We believe that those who do not see as we see or believe as we believe must be mistaken. And with this belief we choose to see things in a way that assures us that our way of seeing things is right. This is part of human nature. However, we can overcome human nature. We can remind ourselves often that we may not be seeing things correctly, and that we never see *everything*. As we do this, we will have a greater willingness and capacity to see things from our partners' point of view.

Validation

Validation involves understanding and valuing our spouse. To validate our spouse we must

+ *Listen* by giving our full attention.
+ *Listen* to the emotions being expressed.
+ *Listen* to the needs being expressed.
+ *Understand* the issue from the other person's point of view.

Reflection

Take a few minutes to respond to these questions:

+ When have you experienced a positive change of heart toward someone? How has it influenced that relationship?
+ What is it like to have someone earnestly try to see something from your point of view?
+ What steps do you take (or will you take) to see things from your partner's point of view?

Weed Eaters Are Not for Marriage Gardens

Attempting to remove weeds from your marriage garden with a gasoline- or electric-powered weed-eater is not the best way to deal with problems and differences. That's because weed eaters destroy everything in their path. Weeding our marriage gardens is a delicate process that requires a gentler, more discerning approach.

Good gardeners know that in order to remove weeds permanently rather than just hack them down a few inches to where they'll grow up again even faster, the weeds must be pulled out by hand. This takes longer, but the results are much better for the well-being of the garden.

Another key aspect of effective marriage garden weeding is that we need to learn to weed our own sides of the garden. Too often we are tempted to focus on removing the weeds from our partners' side of the garden. This usually leads to resentment and additional problems.

Most of us probably would not appreciate it if our neighbor came over one day and started pruning our trees, removing our hedges, and planting a variety of flowers they were fond of in our yard. Although there may be times where we would appreciate some help in our marriage garden, we are most likely to accept that help when we have first asked for it, rather than when it comes as an unsolicited attempt to change our gardens.

Weed-Eater Techniques

When differences arise in marriage, there are a variety of *unhelpful* strategies researchers have identified that many couples employ to try to solve their problems. But using these strategies only makes things worse. These might be thought of as weed-eater techniques.

Harsh Start-Ups and Escalation

Harsh start-ups involve immediately attacking or accusing our partners from the start of a conversation. If we go looking for a fight in the way we speak to our spouses, we are almost guaranteed to find one. Harsh start-ups will almost always lead to escalating conflict. That's because when someone speaks to us rudely or in an accusing way we are immediately tempted to defend ourselves and to respond in kind. This cycle of attacking and counterattacking does little to solve problems or strengthen relationships. So a harsh start-up is a terrible way to begin any conversation, especially one where a difficult issue needs to be discussed.

A harsh start-up can take several forms. It may include things like yelling, using a sarcastic tone, or insulting our spouses. For example, imagine that a wife is upset with her husband because he forgot to take the garbage out in time to be picked up. As she goes to discuss this matter with her husband she is not likely to have favorable results if she begins with, "Hey John! You are such a bonehead! You forgot to take out the garbage and now it will stink up our garage clear till next week. What do you have to say for yourself?" John is not likely to answer, "Wow! Thank you for pointing that out, dear. I really do need to be more responsible." Nope! He's likely to lash out at her for one thing or another.

Criticism and Invalidation

Criticism involves attacking your partner's personality or character with accusations and blame. Criticism produces results completely opposite what was desired. Trying to "fix" a situation or someone else by criticizing them almost always backfires. For example, statements like, "You're so selfish!" "How can you be so stupid?" or "I knew I couldn't trust you to do it right!" are very damaging to our relationships.

It is OK to make specific requests of our spouses when there is something we would like to see changed, but it ought not to come in the form of criticism. If we would like our spouse to be less selfish, we might say something like, "I was really looking forward to having a cookie for dessert tonight. Will you please ask me next time if I would like a cookie before you finish eating the whole package?"

Contempt

Contempt involves things like intentional insults, name calling, mocking, rolling our eyes, sneering, and so on. Although contempt is a close cousin to criticism, it is more damaging. Contempt is one of the most toxic and destructive behaviors in marriage. That's because with contempt we begin to see and treat others as if they were less than human. We treat them as if their ideas, feelings, and opinions just don't matter.

For example, if your spouse spills his glass of orange juice on the floor, a contemptuous response might be, "Oh, that was just brilliant! Maybe someday you will be coordinated enough to drink something without spilling it. Until then would you like to use a spill-proof cup like our two-year-old?" Although this response may seem extreme, it is representative of the herbicide we sometimes spray on our marriage gardens while professing to want a great harvest. This simply will not work. Cruelty will never bring happiness.

Defensiveness

Criticism and contempt invite defensiveness. In marriage, if we feel like we are being verbally or emotionally attacked our natural response is to protect ourselves. We put up our defenses. We raise walls. And often times we fire back with critical or contemptuous comments of our own. This does nothing to improve our situation or solve the problem. Being defensive blocks a couple's ability to deal with an issue. Even when one partner feels completely justified in his or her actions, which is often the case, becoming defensive will only add to the couple's problems.

Defensiveness may also involve refusing to take responsibility for our actions. For example, imagine that I use the last of the butter on my toast without getting out a new stick to put on the empty butter dish. My wife is upset by this because we'd agreed that whoever uses the last of the butter would get out a new stick. If I'm defensive, I might take offense at her being upset with me, even though I had not done what I agreed to do. I may say something like, "Why do I always have to be the one to get the butter out? You can do it just as well as I."

Stonewalling, Withdrawal, and Avoidance

You can imagine that a cycle of criticism, contempt, and defensiveness would eventually lead to something still worse: stonewalling. Stonewalling can include withdrawing from interactions, physically or emotionally, and refusing to communicate at all. When couples refuse to communicate about their differences, relationships become fragile.

A common example of stonewalling is giving someone the silent treatment. This really is a form of psychological torture. Intentionally refusing to acknowledge that our spouses are speaking to us is a destructive way of dealing with our discontents.

It is fair in a relationship to explain to your partner that you are emotionally overloaded and that you need to take a break and calm down before you say something you might regret or that you don't really mean. Once you are calm, however, you should return to the conversation. This idea will be talked about later in this chapter when we discuss helpful weeding techniques.

Rejecting Repair Attempts

A repair attempt is any attempt one spouse makes to heal the relationship after it has been damaged in some way. It can be as simple as saying, "I'm sorry. I shouldn't have said that. I love you." A failed repair attempt is when one spouse rejects his or her partner's attempts to apologize and soothe hurt feelings.

Nothing is more discouraging than being told our apology is not accepted. This would be like what could happen when we take notice that the plants in our garden are dry and parched. We know they need water to thrive and survive, so we turn on the sprinkler. But then we notice that someone has thrown clear plastic over the plants. No matter how thoroughly we water, nothing will get through. This is not unlike what we do to ourselves when we harden our hearts toward our spouses and refuse to accept the healing waters of apology that are being offered—the waters we so desperately need to heal and to live.

Negative Interpretations or Rewriting History for the Worst

Most marriages begin with great excitement and enthusiasm. And most marriage partners see their relationships in a very positive light. This excitement and positivity can continue, even in the face of challenges, if spouses are willing to work and tend closely to their marriage gardens. If we start to dwell on challenges and disappointments, we may soon start to feel that the whole garden was a bad idea. We may be tempted to rewrite our relationship histories with negativity as the theme. When we do this, our once-vibrant gardens begin to look more like a patch of weeds.

Unfortunately, when couples begin down the path of rewriting their relationship histories in negative ways it gets easier for them to talk themselves right out of a perfectly good marriage. At first the steps are small, almost imperceptible. But as they continue in that direction, the negativity comes more easily. Couples may soon find themselves hurtling toward divorce court with hearts hardened toward one another, convinced that no one has ever had to put up with a spouse as insensitive and difficult to live with as theirs.

As a therapist, I have witnessed the telling of many negative relationship histories. They often share a common theme and follow a predictable pattern. For example, a husband who is annoyed at a mess his wife created may begin telling himself things like: she is "always" this way, she will "never" change, he doesn't think he "ever" loved her, and he can't be expected to live with a person like that. The more that statements like these are entertained in thought or in word the more they are believed until they become, in the mind and heart of the person who utters them, undeniable "truths."

When we are tempted to use any of these weed-eater techniques in an effort to work through a problem with our partners, it is a sure sign that our heart is not right. We must stop and focus on getting our hearts right (see the first part of this chapter for ideas on getting your heart right). When our hearts are right, it is likely that solutions to our marital problems will seem much clearer.

Automatic Responses and Double-Edged Swords

Unfortunately, when faced with the little (or big) annoyances that are a part of married life, our "automatic responses" can kill our marriage gardens. That's because so many of our learned or automatic responses to marital difficulties are counterproductive (such as the preceding weed-eater techniques). We are primed to voice our discontents, often in critical ways, and defend ourselves rather than understand each other. But it's possible to learn better ways.

In fact, new research challenges the idea that we must express all our feelings of discontent. It turns out that as people talk about their angry feelings, they often get angrier. In addition, when we get angry and chew people out, we damage relationships.

If you are like me, you may have had both the experience of being chewed out and chewing someone else out in anger at some point in life. First, I invite you to think about your experience of being chewed out. Did that experience elicit in you fond feelings for the person who was mad at you? Did you think, "This discussion really makes me want to do better?" Did you think, "I really enjoy this and hope to be able to treat someone else in the same manner some day?" Probably not. It may be more likely that you were feeling resentful toward this person who was treating you poorly. The result may have been that you would be even less likely to do the thing they were asking in the future.

Now, think of a time when you chewed out someone else. You may have felt very justified in doing it (we usually do), but did you feel better afterward? Did you think, "I'm so glad I got that off my chest? Now I can get on with the rest of my day." Did you feel like your relationship with that person was better or closer as a result of what you said and the way you said it? Probably not. It's more likely that you were left with a nagging feeling that you should have done things differently. You may have had a sense that your relationship with that person was damaged.

As it turns out, anger is like a double-edged sword. It cuts both the person wielding the sword of anger and the person at whom the anger is directed, leaving both wounded and in need of healing. Anger is not a catalyst for relationship growth. On the contrary, it tears down and destroys the tender plants of our marital gardens. Usually the best way to deal with angry feelings is to stay calm until we can turn our angry feelings into reasonable requests.

Reflection

Take a few minutes to respond to these questions:

- Why do you think harshness, escalation, criticism, contempt, defensiveness, stonewalling, failed repair attempts, and negative thinking are so destructive in marriage relationships?
- What difference would it make in your close relationships if you chose not to use these weed-eater techniques as a means of problem solving?
- What will you do to avoid and stop using weed-eater techniques?

Creative Problem Solving

Although getting our hearts right toward our spouses is the key to marital problem solving, working through marital problems still requires some skill and creativity. If what we have been trying is not working, let's change our hearts and try something new. We can consider multiple courses of action. We can team up with our partners to identify solutions that will work best for both of us. We can compromise. We can use appropriate humor. We can seek the well-being of our partners over our own self-interest. If neither partner is willing to budge no progress will be made. Cooperation is another key to marital problem solving.

Let's see what we can learn about creative problem solving from the story of a wife who grows tired of asking her husband to bring a large bucket of laundry soap into the house.

Nag No More

My husband thinks I constantly nag him to do things around the house for me. On one occasion, I was eight months pregnant and had purchased an economy-size bucket of laundry detergent. I had struggled mightily to get the detergent into the trunk of my car. Since I was pregnant, I couldn't lift the heavy detergent from the trunk when I arrived home. I asked my husband if he would please go out to the car and bring the detergent in for me. He got distracted and didn't do it, so I asked him again the next day, and the next.

I finally decided I was not going to nag him any longer so I didn't mention the detergent again.

I knew that I could go at least a week or more without washing any clothes. Only a few days passed and my husband woke up early one morning with no clean pants to wear to work. He asked me why he didn't have any clean clothes and I responded that the detergent was still in the trunk of my car.

That afternoon when I arrived at home, the detergent was in the laundry room and he had started washing clothes.

It can be argued that the solution that the wife in this story used to get her husband to bring the detergent into the house was creative. However, it may not have strengthened their relationship and it may have even created some hard feelings between them. Undoubtedly, the husband in this story was unresponsive and insensitive to his wife's initial requests. If he had simply done what his wife was asking sooner, she would not have needed to outlast him. But the husband's unresponsiveness may not be best solved with the wife's attitude of "I'll teach him a lesson."

One message from this story as it is currently told is that if we can torture people enough and make them suffer enough, they will eventually do what we want them to do. In this case it worked, but it creates distance and resistance instead of positive feelings. When creative problem solving coincides with compassion it is most effective in both the short and the long run. Can you think of ways the wife could have shown more compassion while solving the laundry detergent problem?

Let's explore some solutions this wife could have tried that would be both creative and compassionate. One idea is that the wife could have written a note for her husband and put it in a place where he would easily see it (for example, sitting on the TV remote control). The note might read, "Please let me out of the trunk. I've been trapped in here for days. Signed Tide." This use of humor is a gentle reminder to the husband of what needs to get done and it provides the couple with an opportunity to laugh together.

Another idea is that the wife might say to the husband, "Honey, I'm in the mood to take a romantic walk together. Let's have the first stop on that walk be the trunk of the car. Then, we'll see where we go from there."

This is a direct, yet creative invitation to get the detergent out of the car. It is also done in a loving way and it's an invitation to spend additional time together. When we focus on creative and compassionate solutions to marital problems our relationships are more likely to grow strong.

Ideas for Hand Weeding

Marriage researchers have pointed out that there are some important things couples can do to resolve problems in a loving relationship—things that will help us overcome our automatic (and often times unhelpful) responses. These might be thought of as hand-weeding techniques.

Soften Your Start-Up

A soft start-up doesn't necessarily have to be diplomatic and it doesn't have to be perfectly stated. It just has to be free of criticism or contempt. This is crucial to resolving conflicts because discussions seem to end on the same note they begin. If you feel too angry to discuss a matter calmly, it's best not to discuss it at all until you've calmed down. Keep in mind that if your words focus on how you're feeling rather than on accusing your spouse, your discussion is far more likely to be successful. For example, it is not as effective to say, "You never have time for us anymore. You are too self-absorbed" as it is to say, "I am lonely when we don't make time to do things together."

Let's think back to the account of the wife who was upset with her husband for not getting the trash out in time for the weekly pickup. In the example that was given for a harsh start-up, the wife yelled at her husband and insulted him. We agreed that this was probably not an effective way to address this concern. So, how could she address this same concern with her husband using a soft start-up? She might say something like, "Oh honey, we forgot to get the trash out in time to be picked up. It is frustrating when that happens. Can you help me think of a way to make sure that doesn't keep happening?"

In this scenario the wife has taken some ownership of the problem, even though getting the trash out is primarily a responsibility her husband has taken on. She presents the problem as a shared problem, rather than just his problem. She is not harsh. She does not criticize. She also invites her husband to help her consider ways to solve the problem together. This type of invitation has a much greater chance of initiating a helpful discussion than a harsh start-up.

Learn to Make and Receive Repair Attempts

A repair attempt is any statement or action intended to keep negativity from escalating out of control. It is an effort to heal the relationship.

Repair attempts can come in many forms. It may be something as simple as saying, "I'm sorry" or "I love you." It may be something nonverbal like a hug or a gentle touch of your spouse's shoulder or back. One of my favorite questions, and a very helpful one to ask either as an initial repair attempt or after other repair attempts have been made and a positive discussion has ensued is, "Are we OK?" This simple question, tenderly asked, expresses concern for our partner and the state of our relationship. It expresses a desire to make sure all is well. It also creates some space for the conversation to continue if the need is there.

Imagine how the husband who forgot to take the trash out might use repair attempts in response to his wife's concern, regardless of whether she shared that concern in a harsh or soft way. He might say something like, "Oh honey, I am so sorry I forgot to take the trash out. That is very frustrating. From now on I will take it out to the curb the night before. That way I won't forget."

If the wife had spoken harshly about the trash, she might realize she needs to extend a repair attempt. She might say something like, "I shouldn't have talked to you that way. There is no reason for it. Our relationship is more important to me than getting the trash out on time."

Soothe Yourself and Each Other (Staying in Control)

You do not have to get angry about your differences. You can calm yourself and your partner by speaking in a soft voice, speaking nondefensively, smiling, using appropriate humor, relaxing, calling "time out," thinking positively about your partner, and so on.

It has been said that "a soft answer turneth away wrath." Responding to our own or our partner's frustrations in a nondefensive, soft tone of voice is an excellent way to soothe feelings and keep things from escalating.

132

Smiling and appropriate humor can help diffuse tense situations. For example, several years ago my wife and I bought a new mattress and box springs. We were excited when the delivery people from the store arrived at our home to remove our old bed and put our new bed in place. Unfortunately, our excitement soon turned to frustration when we realized that in our raised bed frame, the top of our new mattress and box springs was literally four feet off the ground.

We had not taken into account how much thicker our new bed was compared to the old, and we could not return the new bed. We were stuck. The delivery people chuckled at our predicament as they headed out the door.

Rather than continuing to fret about our situation, my wife and I decided to joke around and have some fun while we tried to solve our dilemma. For example, we said things like, "I hope you don't get a nose bleed from sleeping at such a high elevation," and "I hope you don't hit your head on the ceiling when you sit up in bed," and "I hope you don't break your leg when you get out bed at night to go to the bathroom."

We eventually solved the problem with the bed by removing the wooden crossbeams that supported the bed and lowering it on to a standard metal frame instead. But more important, we strengthened our relationship in the process. Rather than arguing or accusing one another about our problem, we had fun together while we worked out a solution.

Take Timeouts

Timeouts are another important way to soothe ourselves and our partner. Many people think timeouts are for kids, but they can be more effective for adults—if the adults put themselves in timeout, rather than trying to put their spouses in timeout. They use time-out as an opportunity to calm down, relax, and think positively.

An effective timeout should follow a few important guidelines. First, timeouts should be called for a specific amount of time. This lets your partner know when they can expect you to return. Timeouts should last at least twenty minutes. This gives the body time to go from a state of emotional arousal back to baseline. Second, you should let your spouse know where you are going for your timeout (for example, a walk around the block, a drive to the store, to the backyard shop, and so forth). Slamming the door behind you as you leave the house without any explanation is not an effective timeout. Although you may know where you are going and when you will be back, if your spouse does not know, she cannot relax. She may worry about you the whole time you are gone. Third, you should let your spouse know that she is important to you and that you will come back to the discussion (for example, permanent timeouts where you never return to the problematic issue may leave your partner feeling like they don't matter). Fourth, you should use the time out to cool down, to see your role in the problem, and to try to see things from your partner's point of view. Maintaining an angry mind-set and rehearsing all the injuries you received and the things you wish you had said (and intend to say when you get back) will not be helpful.

The Rule of Twos

One creative way to stay calm and gauge your response to difficult situations where you find yourself becoming angry is called the Rule of Twos. Use it the next time you find yourself becoming angry or upset. Here's how it works.

1. Think about and identify your physical responses to anger (such as increased heart rate, rush of blood to the face and neck, tightening of your muscles, clenching your fists, grinding your teeth, and so forth). Everyone has some physical responses to anger and no one goes from calm to angry without experiencing them.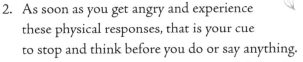

2. As soon as you get angry and experience these physical responses, that is your cue to stop and think before you do or say anything.

3. Ask yourself the following questions. Will this thing that I am angry or upset about matter in two minutes? two hours? two days? two weeks? two months? or two years? (The answer to these questions almost always becomes "no" the further out in time we go.)

4. Some things might matter in two years, but the majority of things we get upset about probably shouldn't matter in two minutes, let alone two years.

5. Depending upon how important the issue is, gauge your response accordingly, but do it calmly.

Compromise

The cornerstone of any compromise is a willingness to accept influence from your spouse. You don't always have to have things your way.

I grew up in home where knives and forks were loaded into the dishwasher with the points facing up. Because this is what I grew up with, I thought it was the only right way. I guess I thought utensils somehow got cleaner that way.

My wife grew up in a home where knives and forks were loaded into the dishwasher with the points down. So, you can imagine my shock when I realized I'd married a crazy woman. After all, I thought, "Why would anyone load silverware with the points down?" That just didn't make sense to me.

When we talked about it, my wife explained that she loaded the silverware with the points down for safety. She didn't want anyone to accidentally fall on all those sharp objects. I had to admit, she had a point. Suddenly she didn't seem so crazy. Even though I still believed that somehow the silverware got cleaner when it was pointing up (which I have no proof of), I agreed to begin loading it with the points down. This compromise created peace and eliminated a little issue from our relationship that was not worth fighting about. I've been loading silverware with points down now for years and the world has not come to an end.

Be Tolerant of Each Other's Faults

If we are not tolerant of our spouses' faults, we will be on a relentless campaign to change our spouses. Focusing on all the spousal improvement projects we wish we could make is not healthy for a marriage. Accepting our spouses for who they are and focusing on changing ourselves is much healthier.

For example, sometimes spouses say things to one another that could be interpreted as rude or insensitive, even when that wasn't their intention. If we jump on our spouses for every little speech misstep they make, they may become reluctant to talk to us. A better strategy might be to give our spouses the benefit of the doubt and assume the best about them.

Silly Girl

When my husband and I had just started dating, I learned an important lesson. John doesn't always mean for things to come out of his mouth the way they do, and I need to give him the benefit of the doubt. My first experience with this was when John was going to run into Walgreens quickly to buy something we needed. But when he hopped out of the car he forgot his wallet. I opened the car window to let him know he had forgotten it. When he returned to the car for his wallet I said, "What would you do without me?" This was meant as a rhetorical question, but he answered it instead. He replied by saying, "I don't know. I'd probably be dating some other silly girl." I had to just laugh. I knew he really meant that he thought all the other girls were silly, and I was special to him, but that is not what he said. We still laugh together about this brief conversation, even years later.

As we conclude these sections on creative and gentle techniques for problem solving, I would like to share with you the story of a couple I know. They were the parents of three young children. The father worked long hours and had little time to spend with his children. Both he and his wife were concerned about the seemingly distant relationship he had with his children. They noticed the children would respond to and obey their mother but either ignore or retreat from their father.

What if this father asked his wife why she thought the children wouldn't listen to him and she responded, "Duh! It's because you're never here. What do you expect?" Or what if this father asked his wife how he could develop a closer relationship with his children and she angrily said, "Spend some time with them, for crying out loud!" We have learned that although the wife's response to both of these questions might be true, it is not kind, and therefore is unhelpful and even damaging.

Thankfully, the wife in this story did not respond to her husband's inquiries about how to draw closer to their children in a harsh or critical way. Rather, she offered a creative suggestion in a loving way. She suggested that any night he was home, he should be the one to bathe the children, get them ready for bed, read to them, and so on.

At first this father saw such a request as unfair. He would have preferred to make bedtime an efficient use of time that would guarantee his "freedom" after the children were in bed, but he decided not only to follow his wife's advice but to put his whole heart into it.

At first, it seemed exhausting. But after three months, it dawned on him that his children were paying attention to him. They were asking him questions about his life and childhood. And they were telling him about their daily adventures.

He quit watching the clock at bedtime and found that he enjoyed the evening tasks better than the freedom he was trying to guarantee himself. Of course he had his own moments of self-centeredness and even impatience, but he became a different person when he put his children first.

Exercise

- What is one way that you have been creative in solving a relationship problem?
- Think of a time when you have worked well together to solve a difficult problem. What did you do that worked?
- Think of a time when you have done well at one or more of the following:
  - Stayed calm in the face of a difference with your partner.
  - Been open to your partner's views.
  - Considered multiple courses of action for solving a problem.
  - Accepted some differences as part of a relationship.
  - Allowed time for change.
- Write a short description of what you did.
- What else could you do to make your relationship better?

Not All Differences in Marriage Can (or Need to) Be Weeded Out

For a marriage to go forward happily, you need to pardon each other and give up on past resentments.
—JOHN GOTTMAN

Not all marital problems can be resolved, but some can. It is our job to accept some differences that may not change and work to peacefully resolve those that can. Diane Sollee, director of the Coalition for Marriage, Family, and Couples Education, says, "Every couple has about ten unresolvable differences. The reason couples divorce is they don't know how to deal with those differences." Sollee says, "Even if you switch partners, you'll still have about ten unresolvable differences." You simply have to learn how to live with some of your differences.

Sometimes when things don't seem to be going well in a relationship, we focus much of our time and attention on the problems. We may even begin to see our partner as the problem. But it's important to keep our perspective during difficult times. One strategy for staying calm and keeping things in perspective is to be willing to overlook some of our partners' faults.

Overlooking Faults

A woman who had been married fifty years shared with her granddaughter the secret of her marital success. She told her granddaughter that early in her marriage she decided to identify and overlook ten of her husband's faults as a way of maintaining peace in their relationship. When the granddaughter asked her grandmother to name some of the faults she had overlooked, the wise grandmother told her granddaughter that she never actually listed her husband's faults. But anytime he did something that upset her, she would tell herself, "It's a good thing for him that's one I will overlook." This simple idea created a spirit of peace and forgiveness in their home.

Differences of opinion, taste, and belief are a part of all relationships. We can accept some differences as a part of our relationships. In contrast, pointing out people's faults and criticizing them doesn't usually inspire them to change or cooperate with you.

It has been said that fault finding is our national blood sport. Unfortunately, many of us spend too much time finding fault with our spouses, rather than focusing on their good qualities and endearing attributes. If we are unwilling to accept quirks in our spouses, why would we expect our spouses to accept quirks (or eccentricities, limitations, or faults) in us?

Reflection

Take a few minutes to respond to these questions:

+ What lessons or ideas in these stories stood out most for you?
+ What is it like to have someone overlook one of your faults?
+ What might it mean to someone else (that is, your spouse) if you overlooked one of his or her faults?
+ Imagine what would happen in your relationship if you spent most of your time thinking and talking about the things you do not like about your spouse.
+ In contrast, imagine what would happen in your relationship if you spent the majority of your time thinking and talking about the good you see in your spouse and your marriage relationship.

Some Differences Are Blessings

Most couples who marry do so because they love each other very much. They have many things in common. They have shared goals and they have hopes and dreams for their future together. However, most couples soon realize that they have a number of differences as well. For example, a wife is an excellent financial manager and her husband is not. A husband is a great cook and really enjoys being in the kitchen, but his wife is less interested in cooking. A wife really enjoys gardening and focuses her efforts on maintaining a beautiful flower bed, but her husband focuses more on keeping the lawn looking nice.

If we are not careful we may let these differences become major sources of contention. A husband whose wife is a great financial manager may complain, "How come you're always so concerned about where every penny gets spent?" A wife whose husband likes to maintain an attractive yard may say, "Why do you spend so much time on the yard? There are other things that need to be done as well."

A better choice is for spouses to look at their differences as blessings, rather than as annoyances or major sources of conflict. For example, a husband with a wife who manages money well may tell her, "I sure am glad you are so conscientious with money. You make sure the bills get paid on time and our account balances. That's something I don't have to worry about." A wife with a husband who takes pride in maintaining a nice yard may say, "Thank you for keeping the yard looking so nice. It really is inviting."

Reflection

Take a few minutes to respond to these questions:

- What are some differences that you have with your spouse that you think of as blessings?
- Are there other differences you have with your spouse that you can begin to think of and see as blessings, rather than annoyances?
- What change might it make in your relationship if you chose to see that difference as a blessing instead?

Exercise

Think of a situation or issue with your spouse in which you have often acted poorly. Think how to apply the ideas in this chapter to that situation. Mentally rehearse the new way, and then try it.

For example, you may choose to remain calm when your partner does something you do not like. You may focus on what it means to you to get your heart right toward your spouse. You may decide to accept a difference in your partner that you have been struggling to change. Picture specific things you will do. Imagine the likely response. Prepare yourself to handle any difficulties. In your mind, practice carrying out your plan several times.

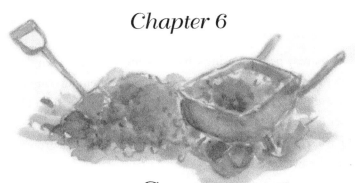

Chapter 6

Serve

Give Back to Your Community

What do we live for, if not to make life less difficult for each other?
—George Eliot

*Service and sacrifice are the highest expressions of dedication and
love because you are showing by your actions that you really
mean it when you say you are committed.*
—Scott Stanley

When our gardens are productive, it's good to share the fruits of our labor with others. Just as you might share your tomatoes and zucchini with neighbors or gather a bouquet of flowers to cheer up a friend, so too can you work as a couple to contribute to your community. Our marriages are strengthened by serving one another and those around us. Sharing our time and resources can make our world blossom.

You may be wondering why we would dedicate a whole chapter to service in a book that is focused on helping couples build and maintain strong, vibrant marriage relationships. The answer is simple—service helps us be better marriage partners and have stronger, happier marriages. Serving helps us grow and it blesses the lives of others.

In Chapter Two we talked about being a healthy and balanced marriage partner, and the three keys to emotional well-being. Service is the third of those keys. Research shows that people who dedicate part of their lives to serving are happiest.

This chapter will discuss two important aspects of service:

1. Serving each other
2. Serving the community

Serving Each Other

We live in a world where individual wants and needs take center stage. All of us are concerned about "me" and "my rights" or "what makes me happy." We must look after ourselves. But if this tendency is not balanced with a desire to connect with others and serve them, then we become isolated and lonely. Happy lives and good marriages involve service and sacrifice.

As we share some of our favorite ways to serve and be served by our spouses, we invite you to think about your favorites.

My wife, Kathie, appreciates my efforts to serve her in both words and actions. I am, by nature, a fairly quiet and reserved person. Kathie, on the other hand, is very talkative, friendly, and outgoing. I think that's one of the things that most attracted me to her. Those strengths that I saw in her were my weaknesses.

One of Kathie's favorite sayings is "to make a short story long . . ." She will often say this as she shares every detail of a story with me about something that happened that day. I love her willingness to talk and share her thoughts and feelings with me. I really look forward to it. I try to serve Kathie by honoring this strength in her—by listening attentively and sharing my own thoughts and feelings, even though this doesn't come easily for me.

I also try to serve Kathie by my actions. Although she works much harder than I do, I make an effort to serve her by doing some things like mowing the lawn, taking her a nightly bedtime snack, helping to put the children to bed, repairing kitchen lights, replacing broken garbage disposals, and cleaning up after Sunday dinners while she takes a nap.

Kathie serves me in myriad ways, but some of my favorites include things like balancing the checkbook, making sure our bills are paid on time, making scrapbooks that chronicle our children's lives, creating quilts to beautify our home, and making wonderful family meals. Her service has truly blessed my life and strengthened our marriage.

Wally and Nancy have some additional and different ways of serving each other. Wally has a degenerative back disorder and every morning and night Nancy rubs Wally's back. Nancy wears tension in her shoulders. Every morning and night Wally rubs her shoulders. For some people these rituals would seem unromantic and unimportant. Yet, for Wally and Nancy, they cause them to feel close and appreciative. These are simple and sweet ways that they serve each other.

Sacrifice: An Important Part of Service

To care about someone does not mean sacrificing one's time and energy
for that person. It means devoting them to the person and taking joy
in doing so; in the end, one feels richer for one's efforts, not poorer.

—Tzvetan Todorov

Sacrifice is an often overlooked and underappreciated aspect of service. That's because as a society we often operate according to social exchange theory. Simply put, social exchange theory teaches that if you do X then I will do Y, but as soon as you don't do X anymore, all bets are off. Although this theory may work well as long as both partners have the perception that they are contributing equally in a relationship, it can deteriorate when sacrifices are called for in marriage.

For example, a couple who are both gainfully employed may get along famously until the husband loses his job. This job loss may require the couple to make some changes in the way they live—to sacrifice some of the comforts they have become accustomed to. If the wife believes that she shouldn't have to sacrifice her lifestyle, or that supporting her husband was not what she signed up for, she may choose to leave the relationship.

Unfortunately, many people believe that when relationships invite or require us to make sacrifices it is time to abandon the relationship. But research says just the opposite. Research indicates that couples who are willing to serve one another and make sacrifices for their partner have happier marriages than those who do not.

In healthy marriages, one partner often gives up something that might have been a personal desire for the good of the marriage. My wife, Kathie, is a great example of this. When we were first married, we had the good fortune to live near her family. We both get along well with her family, so this was a blessing in our lives. I had a good job and we were not anticipating a move. Then, five years into our marriage I had the feeling that I needed to return to school. I was accepted to graduate school in Texas— approximately a thousand miles away from the comfort of our friends and family.

Although my good wife was not anticipating this move, and would have preferred to stay near her parents, we spent the next five years in Texas. Twelve years later we still don't live near family. But we have made many new friends and had some wonderful experiences since making the choice to return to school. I am grateful for Kathie's willingness to sacrifice her preferences in order to allow me the opportunity to pursue my chosen career path.

When I asked Kathie about a sacrifice she felt I had made for her during the course of our marriage, she mentioned two things that were especially meaningful to her. She has always wanted to be home with our children while they are young so she can care for and raise them. She said she was grateful for the sacrifices I have made that have allowed her to do that.

"Even when you were in graduate school, you worked multiple jobs so I could be home with our children." She said she also appreciates the sacrifices I have made to spend time with her and our children. She said, "You spend your free time with us rather than golfing or going out with friends. That means a lot to me."

Service and sacrifice also involve being as concerned about ways we can serve and help as about what we can get out of a relationship. Though it flies in the face of popular American wisdom, constant concern for oneself is very burdensome; whereas self-forgetfulness creates a sense of joy and freedom in relationships.

When we fail to serve our spouses or make sacrifices for our relationships we create a variety of problems. Let me share with you a story from early in my marriage that illustrates some of the problematic effects of selfishness and a refusal to serve.

A Refusal to Serve

When my oldest daughter, Kate, was a newborn, I was awakened one night by the sound of her crying. It was unusual that I heard her in the first place because I have an uncanny knack for sleeping through a variety of noises. And my wife, who is a light sleeper, would often attend to our newborn daughter at night without my even being aware of it. However, this night my wife was still sleeping soundly beside me in spite of Kate's crying.

Upon hearing my daughter's cries, the first thought or feeling that occurred to me was to go and attend to her needs—to serve. But instead of honoring that feeling, I continued to lie in bed. As I lay there, I began to justify my inaction and to shift the blame for the guilt I was feeling to my sleeping wife. Shifting blame is a very convenient way of calming an accusing conscience.

I began to think things like, "What's wrong with her? Why isn't she getting up with our daughter? I can't feed our daughter anyway so what good would it do for me to get up?" I also thought things like, "I shouldn't have to be the one to get up. It's only a couple of hours until I have to get up anyway and if I get up now I won't get enough sleep. Then I'll be tired, grumpy, and less productive all day at work tomorrow. Besides, she's not working right now. She can take a nap tomorrow and I can't."

Notice how when I refused to serve and to do what I felt was right by my wife and my daughter all of my concerns focused on me. That degree of selfishness is a heavy burden to bear.

As my daughter's crying continued, my wife eventually became aware of it. She immediately hopped out of bed and went to attend to our daughter. I did not let my wife know I was awake, but after she left the room I rolled over thinking, "Now maybe I can get the sleep I deserve." However, sleep did not come. My wife spent only a moment soothing our daughter and getting her back to sleep. My wife then returned to bed herself and promptly fell asleep.

I lay there awake, internally griping about how unjust this situation seemed to be and feeling like I was the victim of some mother-daughter conspiracy to keep me from getting enough sleep. It seemed like only a few moments later that the alarm buzzed and I sleepily pulled myself from under the covers. I was tired and I was grumpy. I was on my way to having the type of day I told myself I would have the night before.

At work my mind kept returning to the events of the night before. I kept looking for comfort in my self-justifying thoughts and actions, but there was none to be had. I wanted to be right, but had a nagging feeling I was wrong.

Sometime that afternoon the thought hit me, "James, the rotten day you are having and the poor feelings you are having toward your wife are not the result of anything she has done to you, but they are the result of how you have chosen to see and treat your wife." It was as though a light bulb went off for me and I realized, "I've been a jerk." And even though my wife did not know all the thoughts and feelings I had the previous night, I realized I owed her an apology.

I needed to be sensitive to the trials and difficulties associated with being a new mom. The fact that I woke up before my wife to the sound of our daughter's cries should have signaled to me that my wife was worn out and needed a good night's rest far more than I. I also learned that if I had simply attended to my daughter willingly, like I first felt to do, it might have been a blessing to my wife and our relationship, rather than the burden I made it into.

Willing service in marriage blesses not only those who are served but also those who do the serving. I am grateful for my wife who tirelessly cares for me and our six children. Willing service brings out the best in us. It helps us grow. It helps us be more compassionate. The stories of Keith and Jenny Maurman (who are friends of my wife's family) and Robertson and Muriel McQuilkin are wonderful examples of willing service and commitment.

The Mauermans

Jenny was vacationing with her parents in California when they received a message from her sister back home. The message said, "Something has happened to Keith. Please call as soon as you can." Keith had left for military service in Vietnam not too long after he and Jenny had married. Jenny dialed her home number.

Her sister answered with a "Hello" laced with tears and an emotional quiver: "I've gotten a telegram about Keith."

Before her sister could say anything else, Jenny interrupted, "Just tell me one thing. Is he alive?" Her sister said, "Yes."

Jenny compassionately and hopefully responded, "Then everything is going to be OK."

In fact, Keith had been seriously injured by a Claymore mine. He lost both legs at around the knee. It was months before he arrived in Denver for further healing and rehabilitation. Jenny was there. Practically speaking, she and Keith began planning and adjusting their next steps in life. How long would his rehab take? Should he go back to school? Should she go back to work? In all their discussions, there was no question regarding their commitment to serve each other and look to the future. His injury didn't alter their relationship. They simply faced the new circumstances with an unshaken belief in each other's ability to meet every challenge.

Keith and Jenny have raised eight children. Keith is a hero in the neighborhood. He speaks in public schools. He is certified to teach shop in high school. Jenny works at the elementary school library. It is not that Keith's missing legs are not a reality. It is that their loss has not resulted in anything else that matters being missing from their relationship. They have lived lives of committed service to one another and to their community.

Reflection

Take a few minutes to respond to these questions:

+ What are some ways that you and your spouse serve each other? What satisfaction have you gotten from serving your spouse?
+ What are some ways you serve in your community? What satisfaction have you gotten from serving in your community?

The McQuilkins

In the early 1980s, Robertson McQuilkin was the president of Columbia Bible College and Seminary in South Carolina. He was in his fifties and at the pinnacle of his career. It was about that time that he began to notice his wife's memory slipping in little ways. It was not long afterward that Muriel was diagnosed with Alzheimer's disease.

A few years after Muriel's diagnosis, Robertson decided that she needed his full-time care and that he could no longer serve as president of the college. About that decision he wrote: "When the time came, the decision was firm. It took no great calculation. It was a matter of integrity. Had I not promised, forty-two years before, 'in sickness and in health . . . till death do us part'? This was no grim duty to which I was stoically resigned, however. It was only fair. She had, after all, cared for me almost four decades with marvelous devotion; now it was my turn."

Being willing to serve your spouse in ways big and small will improve your marriage. And research indicates that people who are the most comfortable with the idea of serving their spouses and sacrificing for their marriage are also generally the happiest, most dedicated, and sharing marriage partners.

Reflection

Take a few minutes to respond to these questions:

+ Think of a time when you have gotten satisfaction from doing things for your partner, even if it meant that you missed out on something you wanted for yourself.

- Think about times your partner has sacrificed his or her preference to serve you. How do you feel about that unselfishness?
- What are some of the things your spouse does for you that you have begun to take for granted (for example, making a meal, cleaning the bathroom, fixing something that is broken around the house, adjusting work schedules to take a sick child to the doctor, listening attentively while you share your feelings about an important issue)?
- Ask your spouse to share one specific way that you can give to him or her and then make an effort to give that service.

A Note of Caution

As you have read this section that discusses the importance of service and sacrifice in healthy marriage relationships, you may have thought, "But that doesn't work in abusive or violent relationships."

You're right. Abusive partners will manipulate and take advantage of their partners' efforts to serve and to sacrifice for the relationship. In normal or healthy relationships, service and sacrifice build and strengthen marital bonds.

Although a thorough discussion of domestic violence is beyond the scope of this book, we encourage partners who are in an abusive relationship to seek help. Don't allow yourself to be destroyed by an abusive partner.

Serving the Community

Although serving one another in marriage is of vital importance, serving in the community helps us expand our horizons. The ways in which we can serve are almost limitless. We invite you to use your imagination to identify ways you might like to serve as we share some stories and ideas to help get you started. In this section we will discuss ideas for serving as individuals, for finding a common purpose, and for serving others together.

Serving as Individuals

For some folks, the thought of serving others does not come naturally. Remember in Chapter Three (about nurturing) when we talked about human development in relation to marriage? Infants are not concerned with other people's wants and needs. They are concerned with their own wants and needs. Infants do not think about serving others. They demand to be served. It takes years of development and practice for us to learn to serve willingly and well.

I remember as a teenager I was still struggling with learning how to be good at serving. I remember on more than one occasion my parents or youth leaders enthusiastically planned service projects that they expected me to participate in. I was often a very reluctant participant. One of those projects involved chopping and hauling wood for an elderly couple that used a wood-burning stove as their primary source of heat in the winter. Another project involved pulling weeds and digging potatoes at a community garden that provided food for the hungry. Yet another project involved raking leaves for an elderly lady who could not do it herself.

Although at first I was a reluctant participant in each of these projects (and probably many others),

I was later grateful that I had participated and that my parents and other leaders were willing to persevere in providing me with opportunities to serve. Those opportunities taught me important lessons about the value of service. And something interesting happened along the way. As I served, my mood and my attitude about service and those we were serving changed. No longer was the elderly lady whose leaves needed to be raked a thorn in my side; rather, the opportunity to serve her became a blessing in my life.

For many folks who have worked at it, serving others has become a daily part of their lives. It seems to come naturally. The service is freely given. There is no expectation that they will receive any payment or recognition in return. For those who willingly serve, the satisfaction of serving others is payment enough.

During my teenage years I built up a lawn-mowing business in my neighborhood in Charlottesville, Virginia. On many occasions after work or on a Saturday my father, who was an elementary school principal, would show up where I was working. He would say something like, "I thought you could use a little help." Then, he would jump right in and help me finish a job. He never wanted to be paid anything, although I offered. He simply wanted to be with me and to serve. I'm grateful for his service. I'm grateful for his example.

I will also always remember the kindness of our neighbor, Randy Wright, when we lived in Cache Valley, Utah. Cache Valley is known for harsh winters with significant snowfall. On many occasions when heavy snows fell, Randy would bring his snow blower to our house and clear our driveway. But he didn't stop there. He would also clear all the sidewalks for half a block. The neighborhood was grateful for Randy.

My wife, Kathie, loves to run. She also loves to serve. She combined these activities to become the "garbage fairy." Monday is garbage pickup day in our neighborhood. One Monday morning as my wife was running past a neighbor's home, she noticed that they had not rolled their trash can out to the curb and it was nearly time for the truck to come. So, she rolled their can to the curb. She did this for several weeks in a row before the couple who lived there realized that neither of them had been taking the garbage to the curb. Eventually they discovered it was my wife who had been providing this service for them. They were grateful and they affectionately called her their "garbage fairy."

Severe weather in Arkansas and the southern region of the United States in recent years has provided me with several opportunities to serve those who, in some cases, have lost everything. I remember gathering bags of trash and debris after a tornado ripped through and destroyed much of Dumas, Arkansas. I remember cutting and clearing downed trees in Baton Rouge, Louisiana, in the aftermath of Hurricane Ike and doing the same after a devastating ice storm splintered trees like toothpicks in Pocahontas, Arkansas. I have been grateful for the opportunity to serve.

Wally tells of the way his wife, Nancy, is an inspiration to him. Fairly often she will go visit people who are lonely. She may spend hours listening to them and helping with little tasks. Often she helps them run errands. Inevitably, when she tells about her outings, she glows. She loves using her great gift of compassion to bless people in need. As you can imagine, the people she helps love her dearly.

Finding a Common Purpose

Couples in healthy marriages have goals and ideals that give their marriages purpose and meaning. A good marriage can be built on the pursuit of any number of worthy goals, such as: (1) raising responsible children; (2) being actively involved in the community, school, or church; (3) caring for the environment; or (4) developing shared talents and using them in the service of others. You might take a minute right now to identify some of the common goals that you and your partner share or that you might like to take on.

At this stage in our lives (with six children at home) much of the service my wife and I give focuses on our children, church, and family. Our family mission statement reflects this: "We are the Marshall family and we like to: eat together, play together, pray together, have family nights together, go to church together, be together on special occasions, go on family vacations together, and serve others." Every member of our family contributed to our mission statement and we try to live in a way that meets our family mission. This helps to keep us close and connected in a world that eagerly pulls us all in different directions.

Some couples create a marriage mission statement that helps them focus their service in those areas that are important to them. For example, marriage therapist Blaine Fowers related the story of how one couple's mission to "share their love of Native American art" dramatically improved their marriage.

Wendy and Al

Wendy and Al had been married for twenty years. They felt their relationship had become hollow and meaningless. They sought counsel with Fowers as their last resort before filing for divorce. They did not believe they should stay married unless they could develop an emotionally closer relationship.

Fowers began working with them to improve their communication skills. They also resolved some important issues in their past and improved their parenting skills. But Wendy and Al did not seem to be developing the deep intimacy and open communication they wanted.

After several months of counseling, they told Fowers that they had decided to start a business marketing Native American art together. This was an area where they both had a strong interest and a desire to share this artwork. It also seemed to represent a renewed commitment to one another.

A few weeks after they announced that they were starting a business together, they began thanking Fowers for his help and telling him that they thought they were finished with therapy. This came as somewhat of a surprise to Fowers as it did not seem to him that they had ever really met their original goal of deeper emotional intimacy. Fowers honored their feeling that they were done with therapy, he summarized what they had accomplished, and he wished them well.

It became clear to Fowers that Wendy and Al had "found another way besides deepening intimacy to have a good marriage. They found that their joint participation in a project gave their marriage a deeper and more lasting meaning than emotional intimacy could by itself." Their marriage gained a new dimension when they decided to work together toward a common goal.

It was through his work with Wendy and Al that Fowers learned that although therapy helped some, "their connection to each other was made far stronger by their passionate pursuit of a common interest." He also understood that "being able to communicate in an open and positive manner is very valuable, but having something worthwhile to communicate about is at least as important."

Reflection

Take a few minutes to respond to these questions:

+ When do you most feel that the two of you are a team?
+ What type of projects or causes do you and your spouse participate in together?
+ What specific projects would you like to pursue together this coming week (and thereafter) that would foster a greater sense of unity in your marriage? Do these things.

Serving Others Together

> *Life has taught us that love does not consist in gazing at each other but in looking outward together in the same direction.*
> —ANTOINE DE SAINT-EXUPÉRY

Choosing to serve together makes our lives better and our marriages stronger. Research indicates that people who live meaningful lives are those who serve. They may work to protect the environment, raise good children, improve education, or comfort those who are burdened. There are as many ways to serve as there are different people!

Martin Seligman, author of the book *Authentic Happiness*, says that the meaningful life consists of identifying our strengths and using those strengths in the service of others.

Every individual has been blessed with some strengths and every married couple has some shared strengths. Using your individual and shared strengths to serve others will encourage your marriage to blossom.

David and Karin Gill

Our friends David and Karin Gill have always been passionate about helping young people be successful and productive citizens. And with five children of their own, they had plenty of hands-on experience. After forty years of marriage and a career spent selling machine parts, David and Karin decided to continue serving young people together.

They volunteered to be missionaries for their church. Their responsibility was to establish a ministry for young single adults in Stuttgart, Germany. The Gills spent eighteen months in Germany, at their own expense, working with young adults. Although they greatly enjoyed meeting and teaching these young adults, they found a hidden blessing in their service. Their own marriage grew stronger as they worked together to serve the youth of Stuttgart.

Of their service, the Gills said, "Being of help to others was the part that was most rewarding to us. But through that process, we grew to love each other even more. Serving together changes a couple. You cannot come away from such service without having changed your own life."

Elizabeth's Friends

We know a couple that wanted to find a way to serve in their neighborhood. As they introduced themselves to their neighbors they found that the woman who lived just across the alley from them was an immigrant widow in her eighties named Elizabeth. When the couple first met her, they felt an instant love for her.

Because all of Elizabeth's family lived far away, the couple committed to each other to provide the support and friendship Elizabeth needed.

Every week during the summer, they mowed her lawn. When they baked treats that Elizabeth liked, they took some to her. Every weekend they checked to see if she needed any odd jobs done—fixing a light, repairing a kitchen drain, or painting a room. Almost every weekend there was some little job that Elizabeth needed done and could not do herself.

Often when the couple went out for dinner they invited Elizabeth to go along. Sometimes they had burgers and sometimes something more elegant. But Elizabeth was always delighted to be a part of the outings.

In fact, Elizabeth would invite the couple over for elaborate dinners from time to time. She regularly shared her baked goods with her new friends. They celebrated holidays together that she might otherwise have spent alone. She adopted their family as if they were her own.

Over the course of years, the friendship grew. Elizabeth had both the practical help she needed and the friendship she longed for.

At first the couple thought of their efforts as a way to serve. Over time the couple's relationship with Elizabeth became an important part of their lives. They loved to hear her tell stories. They recorded her words of wisdom. They learned recipes from her. They were amazed by her breadth of knowledge and enthusiasm for life. They enjoyed her friendship.

After six years of friendship, Elizabeth became ill. She was found to have an advanced case of cancer. She died within a month of the diagnosis. Before she died she gave a lovely chair that she had upholstered herself to the couple. The chair sits proudly in their home. And their love for Elizabeth continues to bless their lives and marriage.

There are many ways couples can be of service to others. The following are some ideas to get you started. Take a few minutes to make your own list.

What Can You Do?

Care for a widowed neighbor

Do yard work for a neighbor or someone else

Care for the children of a young mom while she runs errands

Visit neighbors

Take a friend or neighbor out to dinner

Have a friend or neighbor over for dinner

Swap baby-sitting (with another couple with children)

Volunteer as greeters for religious meetings, concerts, programs, and so on

Bake something for a neighbor and hand deliver it to them

Visit a children's hospital and volunteer to read stories to the children

Volunteer to raise funds for a children's hospital or other worthy cause

Work with your church or local community to collect children's blankets, hats, socks, and so on to donate to your local children's hospital

Volunteer with an organization such as the United Way or the American Heart Association

Adopt a college student (or foreign exchange student) for the semester

Take part in a group service project (locally or abroad)

Volunteer to help with an annual school event (for example, bake sale, rummage sale, senior dinner, or a family night out)

Sponsor a youth event for a church activity

Give a smile

Listen to someone

Volunteer on a 4-H project (Master Gardeners, planning a 4-H fun run, and the like)

Work in the church nursery

Visit an elderly person or someone who is alone

Send an uplifting note to someone (monthly or just occasionally)

Take your neighbor's trash out to the curb

Give a hug to someone at church

Help out financially if possible

Exercise

During the coming week(s), what will you do to serve your spouse and those around you? List at least one thing you will do for your spouse and one thing you will do for others. Make a specific plan and rehearse it in your mind, that is, prelive the experience.

For example, you may decide to wash your spouse's car, make your spouse's favorite meal, or do any small job around the house that your spouse usually does. You may also consider joining a service-oriented community or church group or you may decide to work with your spouse to make someone else's life better in another way. Picture specific things you will do. Imagine the likely response. Prepare yourself to handle any difficulties. In your mind, practice carrying out your plan several times.

Chapter 7

Gardening, Harvesting, and Planning for the Future

Whatsoever a man soweth, that shall he also reap.

—GALATIANS 6:7

We have enjoyed spending time with you in *The Marriage Garden*. We hope that the time you have spent with us has been productive and fruitful.

An Overview of the Garden

Let's summarize some of the key discoveries in *The Marriage Garden*.

+ *Commitment*: Often we get relationships backwards. We act according to our feelings rather than our commitments. When we let our fickle feelings make our decisions for us we can talk our way right out of a perfectly good marriage. Feelings change and if we don't have solid commitments to our partners, we are left with nothing to fall back on. Of course, commitment is

167

more than a steely resolve to stick with a relationship. It is also the resolve to keep investing in the relationship and to prevent distractions from destroying something sacred. It is the willingness to tend to and protect your marriage garden.

- *Grow:* When we are vibrant people, we can bring far more to our relationships than when we are languishing. The keys to being vibrant are common sense even if they are not common practice. We enjoy and appreciate the simple things of life. We cherish the best from our life experiences. We look forward to the future. We use our strengths regularly. And we find ways to serve.

- *Nurture:* Relationships need care just as much as plants do. The needed care is not as much about big, romantic acts as it is about simple and consistent kindness. In fact, one of the most important things we can do to ensure a strong relationship is to tune in to our partners' preferences. Simple things mean a lot—when they fit what our spouses want. Simply making time for our spouses and showing them understanding can help strengthen our marriage gardens.

- *Understand:* We often think we have our spouses figured out. Unfortunately, this leads to a hardening of the categories (for example, "he's this way" or "she's that way"). The key to truly understanding our spouses is to continue to tune in to their meanings and to try to see the world through their eyes. We will never fully understand our spouses, but, as we humbly try, we will find ourselves more receptive to and appreciative of each other.

- *Solve:* Sometimes problems take over our minds and hearts. They can entirely block our view of the good qualities and amazing potential in our relationships. Some problems cannot be solved but must be accepted. Other problems can

be effectively managed as we humbly
look for our role in the problem, avoid
destructive weeding techniques, and
use gentle hand-weeding techniques
instead.

- *Serve:* Serving can add a sense
of satisfaction and purpose to our
lives—whether we are serving our
partners or our community. Even simple
acts of service can make a huge
difference.

This summarizes the six principles
that make for a vibrant marriage garden.
When we honor these principles with our
thoughts, words, and actions, we will have stronger relationships.
When we neglect them, our gardens will begin to wilt and suffer.

Of course, the application of these principles requires
patience and wisdom. They must be applied like a master gardener
who carefully monitors the condition of a garden and judiciously
acts to ensure its well-being. These six principles do not operate in
isolation. They interact and react with one another as we strive to
create beautiful marriage gardens.

Putting the Pieces Together

One of the difficulties in solving problems and strengthening
relationships is that marital challenges don't show up with little
tags on them that say, "This is an opportunity for a little more
nurturing." Quite the contrary. We are often mystified by our

marital problems. We may feel like we have tried everything. We simply don't know what to do next.

For example, maybe your relationship isn't bad. Maybe you and your spouse don't fight much. But you don't feel much closeness either. You wish your relationship were more vibrant than it is. What do you do?

We can give you a very clear and definitive answer to that question: It depends! Unfortunately there is no one magical answer. One couple may need one thing to add zest to their relationship while another couple needs something quite different. The best way for you to figure out what will most help your relationship is to seek knowledge from trusted and reliable sources and then listen to your heart.

For example, you may decide to read a book about marriage (like this one!), you may attend a marriage workshop, or you may seek counsel from a parent or a trusted friend. You may also seek guidance from a trained therapist or a religious leader. Any of these activities can be helpful as you seek to find the right answers for you and your situation.

As relationship educators we don't pretend to know how to solve every couple's relationship problems. What we attempt to do is teach principles and ideas that contribute to healthy marriage relationships. As we do so, we invite couples to pay attention to, take note of, and try those things that seem to speak to their souls.

Each of us is equipped with a personal compass—or conscience—to guide us along life's journey. Our conscience is the peaceful voice inside us that, as we hear principles of truth regarding our relationships, will invite us to be more committed, to complain less, to focus on our partners' strengths, or to serve more. When we ignore this compass, we get lost. It is more difficult to find solutions to relationship problems. When we use our compass well, we bring light and hope to our marital gardens.

As you have read *The Marriage Garden*, what has your heart invited you to do (or stop doing)? Make note of those things and take appropriate action. They are the things that will most bless and strengthen your marriage garden.

Avoiding Relationship Blight

Let's consider what may sap energy from our relationships by considering the six areas of the marriage garden.

+ *Commitment:* Is couple time crowded out by other demands like work or children? Do we make time regularly to do enjoyable things together? Do we make a practice of remembering what we appreciate about our partners? Relationships wilt when we neglect them.
+ *Grow:* Are we taking good care of ourselves? Simple exhaustion can poison our minds, our spirits, and our relationships.
+ *Nurture:* Have we figured out how our partners like to be loved? Do we regularly do the things they value? Do we accept our partners' weaknesses? Sometimes we try hard but we're doing the wrong things. If that's the case, we need to study our partners' languages of love.
+ *Understand:* Do we continue to try to know our spouses? Have we studied their preferences, passions, and projects? When we know and appreciate what's in another person's heart, we are more likely to connect.
+ *Solve:* Do we keep problems from taking over our minds? Do we find our common ground and show appreciation for each other?

• *Serve:* Do we serve one another? Do we have causes and projects that we share with our spouses? Feeling that we have a purpose and that we can make a difference strengthen relationships.

The Challenge of Irritation

Let's consider a different kind of challenge. Maybe we find ourselves irritated by our partners. We think they are stupid, inconsiderate, or selfish. How can we apply the principles described in this book to transform our irritation into appreciation (or at least cooperation)?

Again, it depends. It depends on which of the principles we have been neglecting. Let's consider solutions from each of the six areas that might help us deal with irritation. Please consider if any of these are especially needed in your relationship.

• *Commitment:* Sometimes we get irritated because we feel confined by marriage. We wish we were free. We crave excitement and variety. The best solution is generally to bring fresh excitement to our marriages. When was the last time we brought our best selves to our marriages?

• *Grow:* We sometimes feel irritated because we are tired or unhappy in other areas of our lives. What can we do to flourish again?

• *Nurture:* We may get irritated with our spouses because we feel like we are bringing so much to our marriage and getting so little in return. We resent our spouses. We think we deserve better. Almost always the solution to feeling underappreciated is to be more appreciative.

+ *Understand:* Sometimes we get irritated because we don't understand our spouses' hopes, dreams, and challenges. Have we taken time recently to listen to our spouses and try to get inside their lives?
+ *Solve:* Irritation often grows because we dwell on problems. We ruminate. As important as it may be to solve problems, often we simply need to be more mindful of the good. What we give our attention to grows. We can give more attention to the good.
+ *Serve:* Ironically, one of the reasons we get irritated with our spouses is because we feel guilty about things we have failed to do. So we blame our spouses. Clearly it is better to find ways to honor the invitations from our conscience to help and to serve.

The Law of the Harvest: What We Plant Is What We Gather

A man provided a painful and realistic depiction of marriage in a question he submitted to an online family service.

> After 13 years of marriage, I've come to realize that I really don't like my wife. She is everything that I despise in a wife and a person. I'm a religious man, have tried everything the books say, and have taken direct orders from our pastor to implement actions all in an effort to cause a positive change in the marriage. The bottom line is, I see no positive aspects to my wife's personality, and it taints all of her relationships, especially ours. I really dislike being around her and I've run out of solutions. Just short of divorce, is there anything that can be done as a final effort to salvage this marriage? (from BC in NM)

173

We don't know the man who wrote the question nor do we know the wife of whom he spoke. We don't know about their separate life histories, or their combined relationship history. So we cannot speak with confidence about the problems and solutions for BC in NM. But we can imagine some possibilities.

Presumably there were many things BC liked about his wife in the early days of their relationship. Otherwise it is unlikely they would have chosen to get married. Probably most of those good things BC liked about his wife have not entirely disappeared. So, why is he now so totally discontented? One possibility is that BC has turned his attention from those good things to the things that irritate him. He is now focused on the problems that he ignored in the early days of the relationship when positive feelings prevailed.

Maybe BC has also been planting weed seeds in his marriage garden. As he has focused on his wife's faults and his own unhappiness, he may have become far less pleasant and far more judgmental. He may be doing many things to provoke what he dislikes in his wife. Can you imagine living with someone who has the feelings about you that he describes?

We have reason to suppose, based on his accusatory description of his wife, that he expected their marital garden to become lush and productive without investing steady and patient care. Now, thirteen years later, he has a patch of weeds. He is ready to give up.

You can see the law of the harvest at work here. We reap what we sow. Neither a lush garden nor a great marriage happens without lots of work. If we halfheartedly and occasionally invest in our garden, our harvest will be poor. If we make earnest and informed efforts over time, we are likely to have a bounteous harvest. Although BC described his effort to rescue the relationship by reading books and implementing directives from his pastor, nothing will work as long as the soil in his soul is hard.

If BC can soften his heart by remembering good times and cultivating new understanding of his wife in his mind, then the good counsel he had gotten could take root. But, as long as his heart and mind remain hard and impenetrable, no seeds of hope or relationship growth stand a chance.

Most of us have smaller, garden-variety discontents. Maybe we are bothered by a spouse who picks her fingernails or talks too much or watches too much TV. The guaranteed way to make marriage worse is to think and talk endlessly about those irritations.

Would you rather be married to someone who is an exacting accountant and precise taskmaster or someone who appreciates your qualities and accepts your humanness? As we offer such graciousness to our partners, we are preparing the soil to receive seeds of companionship, growth, and happiness back to us in turn.

Resources to Strengthen Your Marriage

We should warn you that not all advice is created equal. Much of the marital advice we hear is simply popular wisdom. Sometimes that popular wisdom really is wise and helpful, but sometimes it's mere foolishness. Some experts are charismatic but unwise, whereas other experts may be more sober but grounded in wisdom. Some books have great covers and tag lines but are filled with impractical counsel. You get the idea. No matter how popular or attractive the advice, you must test it in the laboratory of your own life and marriage. It can also be tested for its scholarly support.

For example, John Gottman is one of the most respected marriage researchers in the world. His books may not be as entertaining or as popular as some in the marriage market, but his recommendations are sound and founded on decades of careful research. There are several other marriage scholars who have also offered sensible advice. Some of their books are listed in the Recommended Resources at the end of this book.

After establishing that the marital advice you've heard comes from a respected source, there is still a two-part test you should apply to any suggestion you are considering using: (1) Does the advice sound practical—as if it would actually work for you and your spouse? And (2) Does the advice show compassion for both you and your spouse?

Unfortunately, many of the old marital prescriptions failed to meet the compassion criteria. For example, it was common some decades ago to process differences through fair fighting. This involved sharing your discontents, but doing it in "fair and civil ways." The problem with this approach is that it keeps people stuck in their problems and it doesn't show compassion for your partner or the human condition. We all have faults. No amount of fair fighting will remove that reality. Rather than discuss problems endlessly, we can turn our attention to our strengths.

Anyone who is determined to have a glorious garden expects to invest time and energy to keep learning and to keep their garden healthy. We recommend that you implement the good ideas discussed in this book and that you keep learning.

Although some very popular programs and books offer poor counsel, there are others based on decades of careful research. Again, we suggest that you refer to our Recommended Resources.

In addition to reading good books, we recommend that you learn from the experience of successful couples. Maybe you know a few couples who seem to have great marriage gardens. You might get together with them and ask what they have learned from years of cultivating healthy relationships.

You might also organize classes or discussion groups where people can share ideas and learn from each other. You might also attend marriage programs and retreats.

Creating a New Future

Regardless of your current starting point, creating a new future together will require planning and effort. Imagine a man who had two friends that worked in the manufactured-home business. When he wanted a new house, he asked each friend to build and then send him half a house. He gave them no plans. He provided them no specifications on size or style. He left them to design the homes as they would.

A few months later each friend sent the man a lovely half-house. However, when the two halves arrived at the site, they were jarringly different. The rooms did not line up. The utilities did not match up. The roofs and walls between the two halves did not connect.

This is a pretty good metaphor for marriage. Each of us was created in a different "factory" or family. In marriage, two people come together assuming that they will readily connect. But we soon find that our traditions, expectations, assumptions, and ways of doing things do not match up. As time passes, these differences become clearer.

177

Unfortunately, we apply value judgments to our differences: "Your family doesn't care about punctuality," or "Well, your family doesn't care about *people*." Each of us is inclined to believe that the way we have chosen (or been raised) is the better way. And we are tempted to hook our half-house to a big truck and pull it down the road until we can find a better match. But we never match up perfectly with another human being.

Marriage provides us unending opportunities to negotiate everything from when it's OK to snack to what spices are favored in meals. When our relationship is built upon a firm commitment, it can endure—even thrive—in all these negotiations. What a glorious opportunity for accommodation and growth!

It takes strength of character to see errors in a partner's grammar or perceptions and yet resist the temptation to correct them needlessly or endlessly. It takes goodness to see weakness and mistakes in our partners and yet resist the temptation to smirk. It takes humility to be proven right and yet to acknowledge that we all make mistakes. It takes sacrifice to discard or limit the hobbies that prevent us from helping around the house.

Mapping the Future

Part of preparing our minds for change requires us to anticipate the challenges we'll face, and to commit ourselves to respond in new and better ways. If there are issues we have typically struggled with in our marriages, it is likely that they will resurface.

We can create a new way of responding in our minds—one that shows wisdom and compassion. We can rehearse the new reaction mentally. Most of us will need to rehearse it many times to be ready to act in different ways.

Try as we might, we won't do it all perfectly right away. We'll be distracted by our ego, tripped up by our pride, snared by our temper, or sidetracked by pain. So we have to go through the process again. We may need to apologize and ask our spouses for patience as we learn to do better.

Thankfully, none of us need be held hostage to our pasts. Rather than being bound by our flawed histories, we can create a new future by using our hearts and our minds to prepare new responses to familiar challenges. In the process, we create a stronger relationship, and—equally important—we become better people.

As authors of this book, we are convinced that we are better people not only because of our dear wives' great kindness but also because of our efforts to learn to join our lives and hopes with theirs. The principles taught in *The Marriage Garden* are designed to make us both better and happier.

Happy gardening!

References

Introduction

Reader's Digest. (1975). *Pocket treasury of great quotations*. Pleasantville, NY: Reader's Digest.

Chapter 1

Baumeister, R. F. (1991). *Meanings of life*. New York: Guilford Press.

Christensen, A., & Jacobson, N. S. (2000). *Reconcilable differences*. New York: Guilford Press.

Doherty, W. J. (1997). *The intentional family: How to build ties in our modern world*. New York: Addison-Wesley.

Doherty, W. J. (2001). *Take back your marriage*. New York: Guilford Press.

Glenn, J., & Taylor, N. (1999). *John Glenn: A memoir.* New York: Bantam Books.

Gottman, J. M. (1999). *The marriage clinic: A scientifically based marital therapy.* New York: Norton.

Gottman, J. M., & Silver, N. (1999). *The seven principles for making marriage work.* New York: Crown.

Haidt, J. (2006). *The happiness hypothesis.* New York: Basic Books.

Stanley, S. M., Lobitz, W. C., & Dickson, F. C. (1999). Using what we know: Commitment and cognitions in marital therapy. In J. M. Adams & W. H. Jones (Eds.), *Handbook of interpersonal commitment and relationship stability* (pp. 379–392). New York: Kluwer Academic.

Waite, L. J. (2001). Five marriage myths, six marriage benefits. *Marriage and Families, 2,* 19–25.

Waite, L. J., Browning, D., Doherty, W. J., Gallagher, M., Luo, Y., & Stanley, S. M. (2002). *Does divorce make people happy?* New York: Institute for American Values.

Wile, D. B. (1988). *After the honeymoon: How conflict can improve your relationship.* Hoboken, NJ: Wiley.

Chapter 2

Gardner, D. (2008). *The science of fear.* New York: Dutton.

Peters, L. J. (1977). *Peter's quotations: Ideas for our time.* New York: Bantam.

Seligman, M.E.P. (2002). *Authentic happiness.* New York: Free Press.

Wilder, T. (2003). *Our town: A play in three acts.* New York: HarperCollins.

Chapter 3

Baumeister, R. (1991). *Meanings of life.* New York: Guilford Press.

Chapter 4

Covey, S. R. (1989). *The seven habits of highly effective people.* New York: Free Press.

Fowers, B. (2000). *Beyond the myth of marital happiness.* Hoboken, NJ: Wiley.

Ginott, H. G. (1965). *Between parent and child.* New York: Three Rivers Press.

Gottman, J. M., & Silver, N. (1999). *The seven principles for making marriage work.* New York: Three Rivers Press.

Chapter 5

Arbinger Institute. (2000). *Leadership and self-deception: Getting out of the box.* San Francisco: Berrett-Koehler.

Arbinger Institute. (2006). *The anatomy of peace.* San Francisco: Berrett-Koehler.

Gottman, J. M. (1994). *Why marriages succeed or fail.* New York: Simon & Schuster.

Gottman, J. M. (2001). *The relationship cure.* New York: Crown.

Gottman, J. M., & Silver, N. (1999). *The seven principles for making marriage work.* New York: Crown.

Haidt, J. (2006). *The happiness hypothesis.* New York: Basic Books.

Warner, C. T. (2001). *Bonds that make us free: Healing our relationships, coming to ourselves.* Salt Lake City: Shadow Mountain.

Chapter 6

Fowers, B. J. (2000). *Beyond the myth of marital happiness.* San Francisco: Jossey-Bass.

McQuilkin, R. (1990, Oct. 8). Living by vows. *Christianity Today,* p. 40.

Seligman, M.E.P. (2002). *Authentic happiness.* New York: Free Press.

Recommended Resources

Books and Resources
on General Well-Being

Martin Seligman, *Authentic Happiness* (Free Press, 2002)
Jonathan Haidt, *Happiness Hypothesis* (Basic Books, 2006)
Barbara Fredrickson, *Positivity* (Crown, 2000)
Sonja Lyubomirsky, *How of Happiness* (Penguin, 2008)

Read More About Flow

Mihaly Csikszentmihalyi, *Finding Flow* (Basic Books, 1997)

Discover Your Personality Strengths

+ Take the Myers-Briggs test from a counselor or human
  resources person in your workplace.

+ Or take the Keirsey Temperament Sorter at: www.advisorteam.com/temperament_sorter/register. asp?partid=1.

Identify Your Signature Strengths

+ Take the VIA Signature Strengths Survey free at: www.authentichappiness.org.

Learn About Gifts, How to Discover Them, and How to Use Them

+ Read Martha Beck's *Finding Your Own North Star* (Three Rivers, 2002).

Books on Marriage

Highest Recommendations

John M. Gottman, *The Seven Principles for Making Marriage Work* (Three Rivers, 1999). Gottman and Silver describe seven principles that make big differences in the quality of marriage relationships.

John M. Gottman, *The Marriage Clinic: A Scientifically Based Marital Therapy* (Norton, 1999). This book challenges traditional forms of marriage-fixing. It is primarily for therapists and scholars but has a wealth of ideas for the serious student.

Gary Chapman, *The Five Love Languages: How to Express Heartfelt Commitment to Your Mate* (Northfield, 2004).

Pat Love and Steven Stosny, *How to Improve Your Marriage Without Talking About It* (Broadway, 2007).

John M. and Julie S. Gottman, *Ten Lessons to Transform Your Marriage* (Crown, 2006).

John M. Gottman, *Why Marriages Succeed or Fail* (Simon & Schuster, 1994).

Additional Books You Might Find Helpful

William Doherty, *Take Back Your Marriage* (Guilford Press, 2001).

Arbinger Institute, *Leadership and Self-Deception* (Berrett-Koehler, 2000).

Susan Page, *Why Talking Is Not Enough: Eight Loving Actions That Will Transform Your Marriage* (Jossey-Bass, 2007).

Howard J. Markman, Scott M. Stanley, and Susan Blumberg, *Fighting for Your Marriage* (Jossey-Bass, 1994).

Michele Weiner-Davis, *Divorce Remedy* (Fireside, 2002).

Blaine Fowers, *Beyond the Myth of Marital Happiness* (Jossey-Bass, 2000).

Michele Weiner-Davis, *The Sex-Starved Marriage* (Simon & Schuster, 2003).

Shirley Glass and Jean Staeheli, *Not "Just Friends": Protect Your Relationship from Infidelity and Heal from the Trauma of Betrayal* (Free Press, 2004).

About the Authors

Dr. H. Wallace (Wally) Goddard is a professor of family life for the University of Arkansas Division of Agriculture Cooperative Extension Service. He develops programs on parenting, marriage, youth development, and family relations.

Wally has authored or coauthored several books, including *Soft-Spoken Parenting, Between Parent and Child,* and a text on family life education.

He is well known across Arkansas and the United States for his public television series titled *Guiding Children Successfully.* He also worked with Extension colleagues to create the award-winning *Parenting Journey, See the World Through My Eyes, The Personal Journey,* and *The Marriage Garden.*

Wally has been recognized by his colleagues as well. He was granted fellow status by the National Council on Family Relations and given the Career Achievement Award by the national association of family life specialists.

Wally and his wife, Nancy, have three adult children and eleven grandchildren, and have cared for twenty foster children over their thirty-eight years of marriage.

Dr. James P. Marshall is an assistant professor of family life for the University of Arkansas Division of Agriculture Cooperative Extension Service. He is a licensed marriage and family therapist (LMFT) and a clinical member and approved supervisor of the American Association for Marriage and Family Therapy.

James has worked as an educator, therapist, and trainer in a variety of professional settings. He has a passion for marriage and family life education and helping people create and maintain quality relationships.

While at the University of Arkansas, James has been instrumental in helping to secure more than $1 million in funding to support family life programming. He has also worked with Extension colleagues to create several award-winning family life programs, such as *The Marriage Garden, See the World Through My Eyes, A Parenting Journey,* and *The Personal Journey.*

James and his wife, Kathie, are the proud parents of six children. They have been married for seventeen years.

Index

D

Human development. *See*
Personal growth
Hurricane Ike, 158
Hurricane Opal, 51

I

"I love you" codes, 89
"I Was Different" story, 107–108
Identifying strengths, 52–53
Intimate time sharing, 88
Invalidation, 121–122
Irritations: acceptance and
forgiveness of, 102–108;
cultivating tolerance to
handle, 10–11; noticing
your feelings about, 6–7;
overcoming the challenge of,
172–173; seeing the good
instead of, 3–5; "Sports Nut"
story on solving problem of,
115–118. *See also* Conflict;
Feelings; Finding fault

J

Jacobson, Neil, 27, 79
Johnson, Lyndon B., 21
Joubert, Joseph, 57
Joy experiences: hobbies and
other activities as, 50–51,
55; savoring life through,
41–42

K

Kind actions, 90

L

Lawn-mowing business, 157
Liddell, Eric, 52

Lincoln, Abraham, 27–28
Lincoln, Mary Todd, 27–28
Listening: benefits of effective,
91, 96; during calm
times, 92; carefully and
responding to partner's
hopes, 96–98; carefully
and responding to
partner's strong emotions,
92–95; reflections
on, 95, 98. *See also*
Communication
Love: feeling understood to
show, 70, 71–72, 73; "I love
you" codes of, 89; sending
messages of, 64–67;
spending time together as,
70–71, 73
Love language: exercise on,
69–70; how to use
your own, 68–70;
understanding your
partner's, 65–67
Love notes, 66–67

M

McQuilkin, Muriel, 154
McQuilkin, Robertson, 154
Managing expectations, 11–13
Marital stories, 85–87
Marriage: avoiding relationship
blight, 171–172;
celebrating anniversaries,
89; as challenging,
frustrating, and enlarging,
60–61; creating a new
future for your, 177–178;
human development for

Printed and bound by CPI Group (UK) Ltd, Croydon, CR0 4YY

09/06/2025

14685908-0001